Managing People in Commercial Kitchens

Managing People in Commercial Kitchens: A Contemporary Approach uses original research to argue that senior managers (head chefs) should differentiate their people management practices in kitchen brigades from those used in the hospitality industry more generally (induction, socialisation, and performance evaluation) due to the group's strong occupational identity and culture.

The understanding of chefs' work from a management perspective is critical for successful hospitality operations but has been historically under-researched. Chapters provide a detailed account of chefs' work in commercial kitchens from an HRM perspective. Using occupational identity and culture as a vehicle, this book explores the different aspects of managerial work in commercial kitchen settings: general management, leadership, education and training, skills and competencies, managing deviant behaviour, managing stress, and managing diversity (focused on gender segregation). The final chapter looks at future perspectives on this unique working environment and the many challenges arising from the latest developments such as the COVID-19 pandemic.

Providing both theoretical insights and practical applications with the use of case studies throughout, this will be of great interest to upper-level students and researchers in hospitality, as well as a useful reference for current managers in the field.

Charalampos (Babis) Giousmpasoglou manages the MSc in International Hospitality and Tourism Management at Bournemouth University, UK.

Evangelia (Lia) Marinakou is a researcher with many years of managerial and teaching experience at different higher education establishments in various countries (UK, Bahrain, Switzerland, France, and Greece).

Anastasios Zopiatis is a Hospitality Management Associate Professor and Head of Department at the Cyprus University of Technology (CUT).

John Cooper is a PhD holder from the University of Strathclyde. His doctorate research is titled: 'The Occupational Identity and Culture of Chefs and Cooks in United Kingdom (UK) Haute Cuisine Restaurants'.

Routledge Focus on Tourism and Hospitality

Routledge Focus on Tourism and Hospitality presents small books on big topics and how they intersect with the world of tourism and hospitality research. The idea is to fill the gap between journal article and book. This new short form series offers both established and early-career academics the flexibility to publish cutting-edge commentary on key areas of tourism and hospitality, topical issues, policy-focused research, analytical or theoretical innovations, a summary of the key players or short topics for specialized audiences in a succinct way.

World Heritage and Tourism
Marketing and Management
Bailey Ashton Adie

Tourism and Urban Regeneration
Processes Compressed in Time and Space
Alberto Amore

Tourism, Sanctions and Boycotts
Siamak Seyfi and C. Michael Hall

Mountaineering Tourism
A Critical Perspective
Michal Apollo and Yana Wengel

Managing People in Commercial Kitchens
A Contemporary Approach
Charalampos Giousmpasoglou, Evangelia Marinakou, Anastasios Zopiatis and John Cooper

For more information about this series, please visit: https://www.routledge.com/tourism/series/FTH

Managing People in Commercial Kitchens

A Contemporary Approach

**Charalampos Giousmpasoglou,
Evangelia Marinakou,
Anastasios Zopiatis,
and John Cooper**

Routledge
Taylor & Francis Group

LONDON AND NEW YORK

First published 2022
by Routledge
2 Park Square, Milton Park, Abingdon, Oxon OX14 4RN

and by Routledge
605 Third Avenue, New York, NY 10158

Routledge is an imprint of the Taylor & Francis Group, an informa business

British Library Cataloguing-in-Publication Data
A catalogue record for this book is available from the British Library

Library of Congress Cataloging-in-Publication Data
A catalog record has been requested for this book

ISBN: 9780367749101 (hbk)
ISBN: 9780367749231 (pbk)
ISBN: 9781003160250 (ebk)

DOI: 10.4324/9781003160250

Typeset in Times New Roman
by Deanta Global Publishing Services, Chennai, India

Contents

List of figures		vi
List of tables		vii
List of boxes		viii
Preface		ix
Introduction		1
1	The commercial kitchens' structure and organisation	8
2	Occupational culture and identity	24
3	People management and leadership in commercial kitchens	38
4	Education and training for chefs	53
5	Skills and competencies for chefs	72
6	Gender and diversity issues in commercial kitchens	90
7	Kitchen deviance – Banter, bullying, and violence	106
8	AOD use and coping with stress	117
9	Future trends	129
References		147
Index		169

Figures

1.1	Global foodservice industry size (2019)	9
1.2	The foodservice industry structure	10
1.3	Michelin-stars classification	15
1.4	Classic kitchen brigade organisational chart	19
2.1	Theoretical approaches to work identity	26
2.2	Occupational culture elements	28
3.1	The key HRM functions in commercial kitchen settings	40
3.2	Onboarding and talent retention	44
3.3	Kitchen staff motivation tips	46
3.4	Leadership style in commercial kitchens	51
4.1	Opera Dell'arte del Cucinare was developed in 1570 by Bartolomeo Scappi	56
4.2	Images of Auguste Escoffier (1846-1935) and his seminal cookbook Le Guide Culinaire	57
4.3	Timeline of culinary education	59
4.4	Culinary programmes in vocational schools and colleges	63
4.5	Culinary programmes in universities	64
5.1	The balanced competency framework for culinary professions	85
6.1	Barriers and occupational segregation in commercial kitchens	96
6.2	Pay gap between male and female chefs in the US	99
7.1	Forms of bullying at work	109
7.2	The Battered Child Syndrome in commercial kitchens' context	111
7.3	The induction and occupational socialisation process for chefs	114
9.1	Best practices for retail food stores, restaurants, and food pick-up/delivery services during the COVID-19 pandemic	133
9.2	A holistic approach to chefs' shortage	137
9.3	Celebrity chefs' social media accounts	140
9.4	Factors that will shape people management in commercial kitchens	145

Tables

0.1	Examples of chef-related books (1990–2019)	2
0.2	Movies about chefs (1996–2016)	3
1.1	Restaurant classification by menu type	11
1.2	Classifying restaurants by service style/level	12
4.1	Reputable culinary schools	67
5.1	Generic (business) competency frameworks	75
5.2	Hospitality competency frameworks	76
5.3	Culinary competency frameworks	79
6.1	Barriers and facilitators for women in commercial kitchens	104
8.1	Classification of AOD and effects	118
9.1	The future dynamics of culinary education across Europe	138

Boxes

1.1	The youngest Michelin-starred chef	15
2.1	Wage exploitation in celebrity chef restaurants	31
5.1	Shortage of skills in the culinary sector	82
5.2	Top ten skills needed to become a chef	86
6.1	Success factors for female chefs	102
7.1	Kitchen confidential	107
8.1	Anxiety in the kitchen	120
8.2	"A daily beer allowance"	126
9.1	Marco Pierre White	141

Preface

This book provides a detailed account of chefs' work in commercial kitchens from a people's management perspective. The authors have conducted extensive research on this topic over the past ten years. Using occupational identity and culture as a vehicle, the book explores the different aspects of managerial work in commercial kitchen settings: general management, leadership, education and training, skills and competencies, managing deviant behaviour, and managing diversity (focused on gender segregation). Based on the existing literature and the authors' previous research, the book suggests that senior managers (executive and head chefs) should differentiate their people management (human resources management) practices in kitchen brigades compared to the hospitality industry (induction, socialisation, and performance evaluation), due to the group's strong occupational identity and culture. The understanding of chefs' work from a (people) management perspective is critical for successful hospitality operations; nevertheless, this is an under-researched area. This book is unique in terms of scale and depth, providing useful insights in both the theoretical and practical perspectives.

The book's intended international audience is both management scholars and industry practitioners across the world. It covers management areas such as operations, leadership, managerial work, and occupational culture, with a key focus on people management (human resource management). Social sciences are also covered in areas such as occupational identity, culture, diversity, and deviant behaviour in the workplace. Industry practitioners and policy/decision makers can also use the book to develop a deeper understanding of work in commercial kitchens from a people management perspective. The book is also a useful guide for academics, college, and university students – so far, there are no chef-related books that are purely focused on people management from an occupational culture perspective.

Introduction

Research context and rationale

This book falls into the field of hospitality studies and focuses on people management in commercial kitchens, and more specifically on chefs and their kitchen "brigades". For the purposes of this book, a (head) chef is defined as a cook in a professional kitchen who leads other members of the kitchen "brigade", who are also referred to as commis chefs, chefs de partie, sous-chefs, etc., per the partie system (Saunders, 1981a). Fuller (1981, p. 46) states that "the essence of the partie system is the division of work into sections, each section or partie being controlled by a chef de partie" whilst "the team of cooks and their assistants under the partie system is commonly called the 'Brigade'".

DOI: 10.4324/9781003160250-101

Life in commercial kitchens has traditionally remained secluded until the emergence of the recent phenomenon of celebrity chefs (Giousmpasoglou et al., 2020) and their "open kitchens", revealing the previously secret "backstage" (Goffman, 1959) of professional cooking. Indeed, a widespread interest in chefs has grown considerably for the past two decades, as illustrated in increasing media coverage of Michelin-starred and celebrity chefs and the flourishing trend for biographies and other written accounts of both high-profile chefs and kitchen life (Table 0.1).

Furthermore, a key role in the creation, maintenance, and enhancement of chef's occupational identity and culture in a westernised context has been played by the Hollywood movie industry (Wright, 2015), further underlining the blurred line between performer and chef. Hollywood can be viewed as an extension of the celebrity industry, which depends heavily on fans and followers. Hollywood celebrity actors and actresses such as Bradley Cooper and Catherine Zeta-Jones have played roles that portray graphically the "violent and creative chef" character (see Table 0.2).

Notwithstanding, remarkably little methodical analysis has been carried out about the work of chefs (Cooper et al., 2017; Wood, 1997) and, in particular, the social structures and processes (i.e., the kitchen "ideology", symbols, rituals, rites, and myths) that underpin the creation and maintenance of the occupational identity and culture of chefs. However, a notable exception can be found in the work of Fine (i.e., 1987, 1996a, 1996b), which demonstrates how chefs and cooks in the US see their status within categories of self-concept and perceptual images held within society. Yet, unlike this research, Fine does not focus on the high end of professional cooking, where, in his words, "a more self-conscious aesthetic dynamic occurs" (Fine, 1996b, p. 16).

Table 0.1 Examples of chef-related books (1990–2019)

Chefs' autobiographies	*Written accounts of both high-profile chefs and kitchen life*
White (1990, 2007); Ladenis (1997); Bourdain (2000); Hennessy (2000, 2011); Ramsay (2006, 2007); Smith (2006); Simpson (2006); Newkey-Burden (2009); Roux (2009); Blumenthal (2012); Leith (2012); Samuelsson (2013); Lakshmi (2016); Jefferson and Ellis (2016); Matsuhisa (2017)	Ruhlman (1997, 2001, 2006); Bramble (1998); Mullan (1998); Bourdain (2001, 2006, 2010); Parkinson & Green (2001); Dornenburg & Page (2003); Kelly (2003); Wright (2005); Buford (2006); Chelminski (2006); Achatz & Kokonas (2011); Baltzey (2013); Blackhall (2013); Gibney (2014); Austin (2015); Andres (2018); Onwuachi and Stein (2019)

Source: Giousmpasoglou et al. (2020), p. 3

Table 0.2 Movies about chefs (1996–2016)

Burnt (2015) Starring: Bradley Cooper Directed by: John Wells	Chef (2014) Starring: Robert Downey Jr., Scarlett Johansson Directed by: Jon Favreau
Julie & Julia (2009) Starring: Meryl Streep Directed by: Nora Ephron	Today's Special (2009) Starring: Aasif Mandvi Directed by: David Kaplan
No Reservations (2007) Starring: Catherine Zeta-Jones, Aaron Eckhart Directed by: Scott Hicks	Ratatouille (2007) Directed by: Brad Bird, Jan Pinkava
Woman on Top (2000) Starring: Penelope Cruz Directed by: Fina Torres	Chocolat (2000) Starring: Juliette Binoche, Johnny Depp Directed by: Lasse Hallström
Vatel (2000) Starring: Gérard Depardieu, Uma Thurman Directed by: Roland Joffé	Big Night (1996) Starring: Tony Shalhoub, Stanley Tucci, Marc Anthony Directed by: Campbell Scott, Stanley Tucci

Source: Giousmpasoglou et al. (2020), p. 2

What is more, a particularly noticeable trend in the hospitality literature has been researchers' tendency to investigate the hotel and catering workforce as a whole, resulting in a lack of consideration for the particularities of specific occupational groups, such as chefs. Thus, Fine (1996b, p. 1) notes that "for all their potential allure, restaurants have rarely been studied sociologically", although Fine's remark applies more to chefs than to waiting staff to whom sociologists have paid a lot more attention (for example, Hutter, 1970; Marshall, 1986; Paules, 1991). This is possibly due to researchers gaining relatively easier access to the "front" of house "region" instead of the "backstage" kitchen (Goffman, 1959). Similarly, Wood (1997, p. 12) suggests that the vast majority of sociological studies (for example, Howe, 1977; Butler & Skipper, 1981; Mars & Nicod, 1984) have been on food (and drink) service staff where "the experience of food service staff and their relationships with other workers (notably chefs and cooks) have been generalised to the workforce as a whole". During the 2010s, various interdisciplinary studies explored the occupational culture in commercial kitchens (i.e., Burrow et al., 2015; Cooper et al., 2017; Palmer et al., 2010; Zopiatis et al., 2011) and/ or elements of this culture such as bullying and violence (i.e., Alexander et al., 2012; Giousmpasoglou et al., 2018; Meloury & Signal, 2014), alcohol and substance abuse (i.e., Giousmpasoglou et al., 2018; Pidd et al., 2014), and stress (i.e., Tongchaiprasit & Ariyabuddhiphongs, 2016). These studies have helped researchers and practitioners to develop a better understanding of the work environment in commercial kitchens and the requirements in terms of people management.

In summary, the above discussion has highlighted that, although the case of chefs has sometimes been identified as unique (notably in terms of the image of the cooking profession and corresponding motivations to enter the field), researchers have tended to consider the hospitality workforce as a whole, often portraying them as marginal and deviant, and highlighting the fusion between work and leisure (Cooper, 2012). This book is the first attempt to deconstruct this approach and shed light on the "backstage" of this secluded world based on the existing empirical research currently available in the literature.

Book structure

This book is organised into nine chapters, providing a rounded discussion of people management in relation to the occupational culture in commercial kitchens.

Chapter 1: The commercial kitchens' structure and organisation

Chapter 1 begins with an overview of the global foodservice industry and a brief history of the culinary arts from ancient Greece to the modern ages. Then we introduce the different types of commercial kitchens from traditional brigade structures to fine dining contemporary restaurants and smaller restaurants, catering, and institutional kitchens. The kitchen structures, organisation, and tasks are explored based on the type and size of the commercial kitchen. The connection between kitchen management and the wider foodservice industry is also discussed.

Chapter 2: Occupational culture and identity

Chapter 2 conceptualises how chefs' occupational identity and culture are constructed and maintained through both work and social interaction. Chefs' occupational culture is based on the *partie* system introduced in France almost three centuries ago; this regimental and hierarchical system requires strict discipline, dedication, loyalty, and high professionalism. Chefs and kitchen professionals work in teams under the close supervision of the head chef and rely on each other to cope with the pressurised demands of their job.

Chapter 3: People management and leadership in commercial kitchens

Chapter 3 investigates the kitchen structure and operations from a people management and leadership perspective in different countries across the world. For almost two centuries, management and leadership in commercial kitchens are based upon the Brigades system and the principles established by Auguste Escoffier in the 19th century. This regimental system survived until today and is met even in contemporary kitchen settings and high-performing teams. The chapter proposes best practices to motivate, engage, and retain talented chefs and kitchen professionals in commercial kitchens globally.

Chapter 4: Education and training for chefs

With the aim of providing the concerned reader a realistic overview of the status of culinary education and training, at a global scale, Chapter 4 explores issues of interest to industry stakeholders. Emphasis is given to the historical evolution of culinary education and training, the development of the curriculum, quality and relevant indicators, associated challenges, including the questionable value of such an experience, and the existing educational offerings, both in traditional and non-traditional educational settings. Furthermore, the long-standing ambiguities that continue to impede the acceptance of culinary arts as a valid academic discipline are critically discussed.

Chapter 5: Skills and competencies for chefs

Chapter 5 identifies the skills and competencies required for chefs at different stages of their career to cope with the sector's challenges. The development of the hospitality industry has boosted the global demand for chefs. Nevertheless, a skills gap is reported on a global scale for kitchen professionals. Managerial and leadership skills (including the so-called "soft skills") and administrative skills are often neglected for the sake of creativity and efficiency. The adoption of a balanced competencies framework is proposed as a comprehensive way to cope with occupational and industry demands.

Chapter 6: Gender and diversity issues in commercial kitchens

Chapter 6 explores the causes of gender segregation in kitchens and discusses how famous female chefs and minority groups survive in this hostile environment. Working in commercial kitchens was always considered a white male-dominated occupation. The challenging working conditions and the occupational culture are the key challenges for women and ethnic minorities pursuing a career in commercial kitchens. The latest developments such as the #metoo and #blm movements bring to surface phenomena such as sexual harassment, discrimination, and the wider gender segregation in commercial kitchens.

Chapter 7: Kitchen deviance – banter, bullying, and violence

Chapter 7 critically discusses the causes of deviant behaviour and coping mechanisms in kitchens. The physical and psychological demands in the commercial kitchen work environment have led chefs to adopt coping strategies that are not always ethical or acceptable from a societal perspective. Phenomena such as bullying, violence, substance abuse, and worker exploitation are known to kitchen professionals globally. Banter and bullying are also part of the occupational socialisation process in commercial kitchens. All new members go through an "initialisation" (induction) stage before joining a team; the entire team will eventually decide whether to accept or reject the new member. The level of acceptance and adaptation to this unique occupational culture determines the future career paths of young chefs.

Chapter 8: AOD use and coping with stress

Chapter 8 explores the alcohol and other drugs (AOD) use as a coping mechanism to occupational stress. AOD use is a critical issue related to creating and maintaining the negative image in commercial kitchens regardless of the size, place, rating, and type of restaurant. AOD use creates several issues in terms of people management; it affects performance both at the individual and team level and can eventually lead to employee burnout. The early prognosis, training, and mentoring, alongside a zero-tolerance policy to AOD use, can be the remedy for what can be called "the dark side of commercial kitchens". The key to eradicate this phenomenon is to change the deeply rooted occupation culture that accepts AOD use as "part of the job", an easy way to unwind, create bonds among the team members, and cope with stress.

Chapter 9: Future trends

The final chapter explores the latest global trends in commercial kitchens concerning people management. Fast-growing trends such as the increased use of technology and automation, the difficulty in recruiting and replacing kitchen professionals, and the changing consumer habits, coupled with the latest developments that the COVID-19 pandemic brought to the hospitality industry, will change the work environment dramatically in commercial kitchens. The industry's transformation will bring a different generation of kitchen professionals that will require the acquisition of a different set of skills and competencies to pursue a career in this demanding profession.

1 The commercial kitchens' structure and organisation

Introduction

The types of commercial kitchens and the organisational structure of kitchens in terms of human resources should be presented first in order to be able to understand other concepts and the culture of professional kitchens. This chapter presents the history of culinary arts and the origins of commercial kitchens. A discussion of the brigade and the ratings of restaurants is also provided to create an understanding of the sector.

The restaurant and foodservice industry – an overview

Eurostat (2020) reports that nearly eight million people were employed in 2019 in the food and beverage industry in Europe, with Greece (2.5 million)

DOI: 10.4324/9781003160250-1

being among the top on the list of countries with the highest proportion of the population working in this industry and the UK (2.3 million) being among the top five. The restaurant and foodservice industry in the UK had annual sales of $35.4 billion in 2020, with more than 42,000 operators. The foodservice industry in the US demonstrated a 4% growth rate in 2020, reaching $889 billion despite the challenges of the pandemic and the shifting priorities of consumers (Fantozi, 2020); on the other hand the COVID19 impact on employment in food services (Kochhar & Barroso, 2020), was the loss of 750,000 in 2020 (National Restaurant Association, 2020). There were 1.512.110 chefs and cooks in quick service restaurants, casual and fine dining restaurants in the US (U.S. Bureau of Labor Statistics, 2021). At the same time, the global foodservice market reached $3.5 trillion in 2020 (Lock, 2021). Due to rising costs, reduced consumer spending, and market saturation, countries were faced with survival issues in 2019. The pandemic of COVID-19 worsened the situation, resulting in the closure of big chain outlets. Nevertheless, a full recovery is suggested to take place by 2024 (Lock, 2020). Hill (2020, p 8) suggests that the global foodservice market lost $1.1 billion, proposing that "in percentage terms, North America will experience the highest decline of (34.2%), West Europe (29.3%), and Asia (27.2%)" (Figure 1.1).

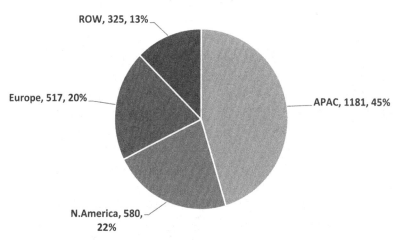

Figure 1.1 Global foodservice industry size (2019). Source: adapted from Deloitte (2020), Foodservice market monitor (p. 11). Available at: www2.deloitte .com/content/dam/Deloitte/it/Documents/consumer-business/Deloitte _FoodserviceMarketMonitor.pdf

Other pressuring forces in the foodservice industry included the instability of global trading and the political and macroeconomic environment challenges, which forced key players in the industry to change their strategies, business models, supply chain, and employees (Deloitte, 2020). This led to new business models, such as more takeaway and delivery services from even fine dining restaurants. It also increased the number of chefs who turned to entrepreneurship and their own businesses (Rogers, 2021), or to even offering "private chef" services (Lucas, 2020). Professional chefs in Ireland dealt with the pandemic through creativity and innovation, as they began reflecting their values, food community, and self-care to inspire young entrants. Their contemporary culinary education empowered them to adapt and innovate, as well as embed their vast array of skills into an open and collaborative sense of community. Evidently, chefs were able to explore new ways for their creativity and talent to shine through. Sweeney (2020) states that "social gastronomy is the new hospitality and the kitchen garden is now an essential extension of the professional kitchen".

Structure of the restaurant and foodservice industry

The restaurant and foodservice industry are part of the service industry, as services are provided to customers. This industry is divided into commercial and non-commercial organisations (Figure 1.2). Commercial organisations include restaurants, catering companies, and others, such as vending

Figure 1.2 The foodservice industry structure

machines. Non-commercial organisations include schools and universities, military establishments, and healthcare facilities, among others. Although the focus of this book is on the commercial sector, it is assumed that people management in service (non-commercial) organisations follow the same people management principals and best practices as the commercial food-service sector. It is estimated that 20% of the foodservice industry is made up of non-commercial establishments (Davis et al., 2018).

There are many different categories or classifications of food and beverage operations. Davis et al. (2018, p. 36) propose that the different approaches include classifying by name, by food type, by business format, by market/direct v indirect, by venue/occasion, by service style/level, and by average spend. In classifying by name, words should describe the type of operations, which is not always the case. For example, "the River Café is actually an Italian-inspired, 1 Michelin-starred fine dining restaurant in London" (p. 36). When classified by food type, the type of food served is the variable used to categorise restaurants. Barrows and Viera (2013) proposed categories such as burgers, chicken, BBQ, Chinese, etc., with an expanded list that is US-centric. Such categories have been recognised based on the menu offered, as illustrated in Table 1.1.

Food and beverage businesses are classified by so many different business formats, such as franchising, tenancy, lease agreement, chains, or management contracts (Davis et al., 2018, p. 40). Figure 1.2 illustrates the classification by direct/indirect operations. Five major categories exist on a mix of styles of service, which are illustrated in Table 1.2.

Table 1.1 Restaurant classification by menu type

Menu Type	Description and Examples
Local cuisine	Restaurants that use only ingredients from the local area and in the appropriate season.
National cuisine	Restaurants focused on national cuisines i.e., Italian, Mexican, Greek, and Chinese.
Ingredient dominated	Restaurants focused on a single dominant ingredient i.e., meat, fish, or vegetables.
Theme concept	Restaurants based on a themed concept i.e., Hard Rock Café, TGI Friday's, Planet Hollywood
Healthy eating	Restaurants focused on healthy eating i.e., plant-based, vegan, and vegetarian.
Cooking style	Restaurants focused on a particular cooking method, i.e., Nouvelle cuisine, haute cuisine, and molecular cuisine.
Chef-centric	Restaurants focused on the name and style of celebrity chefs such as Gordon Ramsay, Nobu Matsuhisa, and Heston Blumenthal.

Source: adapted from Davis et al. (2018, p. 38)

Table 1.2 Classifying restaurants by service style/level

Service Style	Description
Fine dining	Represent luxury dining at the highest quality of ingredients and cooking techniques served with a degree of formality. Often associated with the Michelin star system.
Molecular gastronomy	Describes the combination of food with science using technical advances in equipment and ingredients. Often associated with fine dining restaurants.
Casual dining	Known as "family" dining or "popular" dining, with a relaxed style of service; there are two distinctive types of casual dining restaurants: • Fine casual: relaxed style of service with a refined food offer. • Fast casual: budget restaurants with satisfactory quality of food, towards the fast-food market.
Quick service	Known as fast-food restaurants, with limited menus and automated; in most cases food preparation and orders taken and delivered at a counter.
Public houses & gastro pubs	Licensed establishments primarily for drinking alcoholic beverages, sometimes incorporating the offer of a variety of foods.
Coffee/ tea shops	Orders are placed and delivered at the counter, the centrality of the business is coffee and/or tea and light choices of food/ snacks.
Takeaway	Food is prepared for takeaway only, in fixed, mobile, or popup units i.e., festival and events food stalls. It is not uncommon to combine with fast casual dining or quick service restaurants.

Source: adapted from Davis et al. (2018, p. 43) and Cousins (2019, p. 17)

Barrows et al. (2016) proposed the classification by average spend, referring to the price paid, which is part of the service experience. All of the above shows that there are a variety of different foodservice operations with different characteristics that are considered in the ways that these are managed, thus demonstrating the complexity of the sector. Johnston et al. (2012) suggest that the management of service operations requires constant changes to processes and people being motivated to achieve greater quality of service and productivity.

Commercial kitchens

Commercial restaurants make up the majority of businesses operating in the foodservice industry (Cousins, 2019; Davis et al., 2018). Figure 1.2

illustrates the division of foodservice operations, showing that commercial kitchens are found in hotels, restaurants, conference centres, leisure attractions, private healthcare, and transportation. Cousins (2019) states that restaurants in different forms, such as fine dining, buffets, and cafeterias, are the main type of commercial businesses. Catering and banquets refer to cases where the number of people and the menu are predetermined by the customer. Such services may be provided in a hotel, conference centre, or even outside in venues such as clubs. Demand for contract catering is growing in schools and healthcare in the UK (Cousins, 2019, p. 78). And although the prison population has fallen in England and Wales, catering requests and expenditure increased in 2018 (Cousins, 2019, p. 78).

Retail stores i.e., supermarkets or vending machines, offer prepared meals, or even at stadia, i.e., football, horse racing, golf, and other sports. For example, Wembley, one of the biggest catering sites in Europe (Davis et al., 2018, p. 73), includes a restaurant, the great hall and banquet space, two a la carte eateries and two brasseries, two champagne and seafood bars, and two large free-flow public outlets showing the variety of food and beverage outlets found in a stadium, "making it a complex operation that requires planning and organisation to ensure success" (p. 73). Similar establishments and organisations are found in leisure venues such as museums, zoos, etc. (Davis et al., 2018, p. 81). Food vending machines may sell snacks, sandwiches, or even heated food (p. 201).

Moreover, the foodservice sector includes airlines and cruise ships. For example, in 2019, 29.7 million passengers took ocean cruises (Statista, 2019), where food is available 24/7 with options for fine and/or casual dining, along with buffets and room service. Cruises emphasise sustainability and waste reduction, catering to single cruisers, microcruises, and luxury cruising (Micallef, 2020). Cruise ships have large-scale kitchens with stations that can produce large quantities of food every day; they bake and make ice cream every day, but more importantly, they also incorporate fresh, local ingredients in on-board dishes, as the destinations inspire the menus or house award-winning chefs (Gray, 2019). Ferry catering is competitive, as demand for innovative offerings in food is growing (Cousins, 2019).

Restaurant guides and ratings

Consumers and other organisations classify restaurants on different criteria through guides or other ratings (Cousins, 2019). Several organisations rate restaurants in terms of the establishment, the food, and service, with the most common being the *Zagat Survey* and the *Michelin Guide* (www .viamichelin.com). The *Zagat Survey* (www.zagat.com) rates restaurants in terms of food, décor, service, and cost with a 30-point scale based on people's data from the survey, and hence it is not an official rating (Cousins, 2019). In the US, the *Mobil Travel Guide* (revamped to *Forbes Travel Guide*, www.forbestravelguide.com) rates restaurants on a scale from one to five stars, with those restaurants scoring a five being those that provide an excellent experience and flawless culinary speciality. The largest restaurant and menu guide is *MenuPix* (www.menupix.com), which is a site with over 16,000 restaurant menus in various US cities (Cousins, 2019). The *AAA* is another guide which rates restaurants on a 1 to 5 Diamond scale; this scale is very similar to that of Michelin. There is also another guide for pubs known as the *AA Restaurants and Pub Guide* (www.theaa.com /getaway/restaurant_home.jsp) (Cousins, 2019, p. 47). In terms of "novelty" and "innovation", another guide, the *World's 50 Best Restaurants List*, has been available since 2002 and is based on the voting of gastro experts. Similarly, the *Pellegrino*'s guide differentiates listing by continent and publishes the *Best 100 Restaurants* of the world list. Other ways for obtaining restaurant ratings include consumers' reviews, food critics, and food bloggers who may influence people's choices of restaurant.

The *Michelin Guide* is more popular in Europe, with a reputation expanding to other parts of the world. The criteria include quality of product, mastery of flavours, cooking mastery, personality of the cuisine, value for the price, and consistency, with ratings from one to three stars (Cousins, 2019; Davis et al., 2018; Bouty & Gomez, 2013). This is considered to be the "red book" since its beginning in 1926, when only one star was awarded (Murphy, 2015). After 1931, two and three stars were added (Donnet, 2008). According to the guide, one star means "excellent restaurant in its category", two stars mean "excellent cooking worth a detour", and three stars is reserved for "exquisite cuisine, worth a special journey" (Michelin, 2006). In 2014, only 6 women out of 110 chefs had earned three stars (Haddaji et al., 2017) (Figure 1.3).

Anonymous inspections and independence are the way in which hotels and restaurants are evaluated (Bouty & Gomez, 2013). The review is done annually by a secret diner, in high secrecy, thus making every meal potentially the one to be a perfect display of the restaurant's skills (Gonzalez, 2019). The guide is published annually, recognising cultural differences among 21 countries worldwide (Michelin, 2017; Eren & Guldemir, 2017). It also includes a written description of each locale and other symbols

✿
"A very good restaurant in its category"
Une très bonne table dans sa catégorie

✿✿✿
"Excellent cooking, worth a detour"
Table excellente, mérite un détour

✿✿✿
"Exceptional cuisine, worth a special journey"
Une des meilleures tables, vaut le voyage

Figure 1.3 Michelin-stars classification. Source: adapted from Michelin (2006). Photo credits: Jametlene Reskp (unsplash.com)

to provide more information on the operation's ambiance, type of cuisine, specialties, and wine list. Subakti (2013) adds that the guide provides ratings of one to five forks and spoons for restaurants and one to five pavilions for hotels, demonstrating considerations of décor, service, cleanliness, and service.

BOX 1.1 THE YOUNGEST MICHELIN-STARRED CHEF

A. Chaniotis: The youngest Michelin-starred Greek chef!

Aged just 28, Asimakis Chaniotis has become the youngest Michelin-star chef in London and one of the first two Greeks outside of Greece to receive this prestigious accolade.

About two years ago, Pied à Terre, one of the best restaurants in London, announced the appointment of Athens born and raised Asimakis Chaniotis as its new Head Chef. Having served as sous chef under both Marcus Eaves and Andy McFadden, Asimakis, aged just 28, brings a fresh vision for the future and yet another Michelin star to the critically-acclaimed French restaurant.

"I think that the most popular dish – and my personal favorite – is the smoked quail with celeriac, truffle, roasted hazelnuts, Parmigiano and confit egg yolk. My favorite ingredient is foie gras".

"At this moment, my main goal is to maintain my Michelin star and get a second one, here in London. In the long run, I could, of course, see myself opening my own restaurant in my hometown, Athens. In fact, I would like that very much".

Donou (2019)

Marco Pierre White described the pressure of the Michelin guide, as it can make or break careers, restaurants, or even entire towns. A three-starred Michelin restaurant may be a monument for a place, expressing the art of cooking. Such restaurants bring publicity, more business, and profitability, but they also bring pressure, high expectations, and risk (Gonzalez, 2019). For this reason, White gave back his stars, asking to be removed from guidebooks. Bernard Loiseau committed suicide in 2003 in France from the pressure he felt regarding rumours that he might lose stars. His restaurant retained its three stars, and dinner was served the day he died, indicating that serving customers was a priority over grieving (Sitwell, 2012).

The structure of commercial kitchens

The organisation and hierarchy in commercial kitchens is locked to an antiquated system that can be traced back to 18th century pre-revolutionary France, when Francois Vatel introduced the partie system (Balazs, 2001). The essence of the *partie* system is the division of work into sections, with each section or partie being supervised by a *chef de partie* who is a craft specialist. All of the parties come under the command of the *chef de cuisine* (head chef), who is assisted by one or more *sous chefs* (Cousins, 2019). The team of cooks and their assistants under the partie system is commonly known as the kitchen "brigade" (Balazs, 2001). The militaristic hierarchy of the partie system, strict discipline and strong solidarity that prevail within the occupational group, is evident in many chefs' biographies (i.e., White, 1990, 2006; Bourdain, 2000; Ramsay, 2006). Wood (1997, p. 85) argues that the partie system persists in many hotels and restaurants (including smaller units) because its emphasis on specialisation helps guarantee interdependency and teamwork, whilst fostering "individual skill and responsibility that allows for controlled creativity within a bureaucratic work structure*"*.

Evidently, professional kitchens operate in an organised way following a hierarchy named the *Brigade de Cuisine* (Gonzalez, 2019), a system created by Georges-Auguste Escoffier (a famous French chef) who based it on the military hierarchy and the Efficiency Movement (known as Taylorism and Scientific management) (Fuhrmeister, 2015). This system focuses on a strict chain of command and delegation of tasks, which creates a culture that is found to be the reason behind the poor health of restaurant workers (Twatchman, 2017). Bourdain (2010) described this culture as an abusive system that was not designed to uplift or educate, but rather to push and pressurise. A growing number of chefs are rejecting this culture and the hierarchy of the brigade, as they do not want to work in abuse and stress, and they rather like more flexibility, collaboration, and enjoyment from work (Twatchman, 2017). Agg (2017) proposes that tight bonds and working conditions in the kitchen lead cooks to consider colleagues as family, which then contributes to loyalty. The "family meal" is an exhibition of how the family culture is found in the brigade, with the meal being prepared for kitchen staff before the restaurant opens for service.

The brigade system helps kitchens to be organised, as everyone knows their role. Each cook is given specific tasks based on their experience and expertise, people in the kitchen are divided into teams, and the head chef has the role of commander in chief, just like the military and as per the Efficiency Movement guidelines (Gonzalez, 2019). Interestingly, Escoffier (1987) adopted four main principles from Taylor's theory in his brigade:

1. Replace rules of thumb with science, creating organised knowledge;
2. Achieve cooperation of human beings over chaotic individualism;
3. Work for maximum output;
4. Develop all workers to the fullest extent possible for their own, and the company's, highest prosperity.

These principles enabled restaurants to serve customers quickly, maximising their production with emphasis placed on output, structure, and efficiency. A sense of order and professionalism is created by such rigid rules which will unify and institutionalise staff. Moreover, the brigade system was used as an educational system for order and discipline (Lee, 2014). The brigade system has remained in use for more than 100 years in fine dining, cultivating practices and cultures that define the dynamics in the kitchen and the structure of the workday. Bourdain (2000), in support of the system, views it as a necessary structure that helps the workday's flow. Some criticism on the system refers to the rigidness and the strict division of work which does not allow improvisation, flexibility, creativity, and/or support when a cook is ill. In addition, it is correlated to the stress and pressure found in modern restaurant work and is associated with health issues in the profession (Cullen, 2012).

The kitchen brigade structure

The structure and size of the brigade depend on the type of restaurant and its size. Harris and Giuffre (2015, p. 18) base the hierarchy in

> the fact that chefs have traveled a long road to arrive at the professional status they receive today. For much of their history, chefs have

been seen as a form of blue-collar manual labor. It has been quite the journey from the 'chef as servant' mentality to the idea of 'chefs as the new rock stars', complete with television shows, lucrative product lines, and international restaurant empires.

It took a lot of time, effort, and hard work for chefs to be acknowledged, as their creations "were seen to belong to their employers and were adding to the restaurant owner's status" instead of being "an expression of their own creativity and taste" (Harris & Giuffre, 2015, p. 20). Bourdain (2004) provided his own groups of kitchen workers, the "artists" who are in the minority and are high-maintenance individuals, the "specialists" which included patissiers and butchers, and the "exiles" who are people that could not make it in any other job, which included the "misfits" in reference to immigrants.

Organisational power structures define the hierarchy in the kitchen, with the head chef leading the team. Organisational systems identify how the work is distributed, but in general, the most typical positions include the Executive Chef, Chef de Cuisine (Head Chef), Sous Chef (Deputy Chef), Chef de Partie (Station Chef), Commis Chef (Junior Chef), Kitchen Porter, Escuelerie (Dishwasher), and the Aboyeur (Waiter/Waitress).

The structure of a typical brigade is presented in Figure 1.4. It would be beneficial to provide the distinction between chef and cook, which is, according to Gay (2017, p. 19):

- A chef is trained to master culinary forms, but also to provide creative innovation in menu, preparation, and presentation;
- A cook is trained to master forms of food preparation, but usually takes close direction from a chef.

Executive chef

This is the highest position with a managerial role, as they are not usually responsible for cooking, but rather for operating and managing different outlets. In most restaurants, the executive chef is the owner, or otherwise reports directly to the owner, of the restaurant (Davis et al., 2018).

Chef de cuisine (head chef)

This position is the highest in the kitchen when there is no executive chef. The head chef is responsible for all of the food coming out of the kitchen, as well as mentoring the sous chef. Ferguson (2004) claimed that the "chef

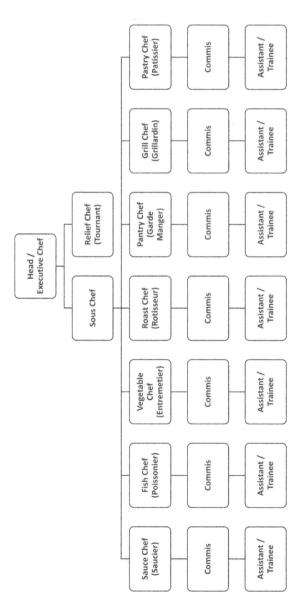

Figure 1.4 Classic kitchen brigade organisational chart

de cuisine" originated from the military title "officer de cuisine". Allen and Mac Con Iomaire (2017) state that a small kitchen may have only one head chef, whereas in a large hotel, two or three head chefs may be found in different kitchens. Harrington (2005) proposed that the head chef is the CEO, and that the team are the board of directors in the kitchen. In their study, Allen and Mac Con Iomaire (2017) propose the demographics and background of a head chef, showing the multifaceted roles that a head chef may possess. Chefs enter their profession from the bottom, as any other manager does. For example, Balazs (2002) found that three-star Michelin chefs in France are charismatic, attract loyalty, and motivate their team to work long hours, sometimes without extra pay, just for the feeling of doing something great. Chefs demonstrate diverse training and educational backgrounds; for example, Heston Blumenthal, Gordon Ramsay, and Raymond Blanc all became successful chefs in the UK without any prior college or apprenticeship training. Their determination, hard work, and drive were the keys to their success (Allen & Mac Con Iomaire, 2017).

Sous chef (deputy chef)

The second in hierarchy is the sous chef, who is usually training to become head chef (Gonzalez, 2019). For this position, the sous chef is responsible for various stations, day-to-day operations, and deputises the head chef. Depending on the size of the kitchen, there may be more than one sous chef in place. They may lead kitchen staff, but they cook mainly to assist or expedite the food from the kitchen to the wait staff.

Chef de partie (station chef)

Different roles are found at this level, as they include responsibility for different stations in the kitchen working on meat, fish, etc. Gonzalez (2019) states that in the US, these are known as line cooks. They do most of the cooking in a kitchen.

Commis chef (junior chef)

Under the chef de partie, the commis chef is trained on a specific station and aspires through gaining experience to become a chef. They are responsible for most of the major tasks, such as chopping vegetables, making stocks, or perhaps assisting the chef de partie during meal service (Gonzalez, 2019).

Stagiaries (stages)

These are trainees or interns in the kitchen who work in a particular restaurant for a specific period of time (either paid or unpaid). They may be professional cooks who undertake a stage for learning another type of cuisine or cooking. In this case, they receive the opportunity to develop networks and perhaps obtain future jobs, or they may be students at culinary schools who have to work as part of their curriculum (Marinakou & Giousmpasoglou, 2020; Gonzalez, 2019).

Kitchen porter

This role involves assistance with tasks in the kitchen, i.e., in food preparation or some cleaning duties.

Escuelerie (dishwasher)

Responsible for any washing used for cooking and food preparation in the kitchen.

The brigade system is useful for large restaurants, but most foodservice business and service establishments today cannot support such a large number of staff in the kitchen, due to the popularity of casual dining, labour cost, and size.

Kitchen operations

Quality of service is not confined to a particular type of restaurant, service style, or kitchen organisation (Cousins, 2019). Managers in foodservice operations should reinforce and support staff in maintaining good standards of service. Teamwork and collaboration with staff in different sections is vital to the successful operation of such businesses (as is discussed in Chapter 3). Davis et al. (2018, p. 49) define fine dining restaurants as "those establishments that offer very high standards in all aspects of operation.... They can be found in 4 and 5 star hotels or as free-standing restaurants". These restaurants cater for the "eating-out market that demands the highest standards" (p. 50). They are profit-oriented with implications on food cost which require careful calculation of the price level and volume of sales. Such operations depend on the demand, as they are "characterised by the need for high capital,... have high percentage of fixed costs, their product is perishable and a demand for that product that is unstable" (p. 51).

Staffing of fine dining restaurants shows changes over the years. A chef may be the owner and manager of such a restaurant, but with a more traditional organisation in the kitchen, where a sous chef is responsible for the operations. Communication of staff in the kitchen with service staff is important. Electronic Point of Sale (EPOS) supports communication to ensure that the food is served at the quality it is cooked at, reduces the time to place the order in the kitchen, and helps the kitchen be organised in terms of dishes to be prepared (Davis et al., 2018). Routines and rituals are established when the food is prepared, the hours are put in at work, and busy shifts take place (Bloisi & Hoel, 2008). The culture and working conditions in kitchens are described in Chapter 3; however, it is useful to discuss some issues in order to understand the structure and organisation of commercial kitchens. Most of the included activities are time consuming, i.e., a cutting board may be used for three different purposes, and has to be washed and reused each time (Bloisi & Hoel, 2008). Chefs have to have "skillful hands", tacit knowledge, and follow practices which contain "learning with traces of materiality, language, symbols and social structures" (Wellton et al., 2019, p. 404). People in the kitchen use their own language and expressions, i.e., "behind" and "hot"; or head chefs use written lists of dish descriptions, inviting staff to express opinions, participate in decision making, and "they are less likely to feel humiliated after making a mistake" (p. 419). As commercial kitchens employ a large number of immigrants from different countries, a "co-created language contributes to unity and bonding facilitating communication and efficiency" (Gonzalez, p. 30).

Structural changes are found in the foodservice industry starting from the "Fair Kitchens Project" by Unilever in 2018, putting together a code of ethics, inspiring staff, and breaking barriers related to gender, ethnicity, and religion under the statement of "a kitchen culture that's kinder and more open than the one we know" (Gonzalez, 2019, p. 66). Other changes include the need for increased wages, raising minimum wage, and bringing back tipping in the US (Oatman, 2017). Flexible work schedules are also required, especially with the impact of crises and the pandemic on the hospitality and tourism industry, supporting better structures, processes, and resources (Oatman, 2017).

Sweeney (2020) adds that self-care is a priority for chef sustainability for the professional mindful chef. The separation of the kitchens from the service area is found to be important, as consumers do not want to see the unpleasant work that often occurs in food preparation or the impact of people's views of men and women cooking. Even in open kitchen arrangements, cooking is more of a role play than a true representation of hard labour that is found in professional cooking (Harris & Giuffre, 2015, pp. 27–28). Research on chefs has focused on closed kitchens, documenting the prevailing masculine world of work (Giousmpasoglou et al., 2018) and highlighting the need for more research on open kitchens in order to provide a deeper understanding of the changes that open kitchens have brought to the profession. The socialisation process has created a work culture of collective belonging (Barker, 2018). Modern culinary and nouvelle cuisine brought the need for co-creation with the customer and visual interaction to the dining experience, not only with the front-line staff, but also with the kitchen staff (Graham et al., 2020). Staff are the actors of a "theatre", but "co-creation can only take place if there are systems in place to facilitate this engagement" (Graham et al., 2020, p. 28). These kitchens are a growing trend which reassures customers that their food is prepared and cooked, and that hygiene is maintained. This trend has also forced chefs to adapt through combining a front-stage performance to meet the expected societal norms, and has created a new self from the embodied social interaction with customers.

Conclusion

This chapter provided an understanding of the challenges, issues, and trends in commercial kitchens. It also demonstrated the brigade system by examining its origins, culture, and the way it is organised in modern kitchens. The kitchen brigade of the future looks different from the brigade of the past, with the size and structure of restaurants determining the size of the brigade and tasks performed (see also Chapter 9). These changes are also expected to affect people management in commercial kitchens.

2 Occupational culture and identity

Introduction

A particularly noticeable trend in the hospitality literature has been the researchers' tendency to investigate the hotel and catering workforce as a whole, which has therefore resulted in a lack of consideration being given to the particularities of specific occupational groups, such as chefs, cooks, and commercial kitchen workers. It is not surprising therefore that little methodical analysis has been carried out about the work of chefs (Alexander et al., 2012; Cooper et al., 2017; Wood, 1997) and, in particular, the social structures and processes (i.e., the kitchen "ideology", symbols, rituals, rites, and myths) which underpin the creation and maintenance of the occupational identity and culture of chefs (Palmer et al., 2010).

DOI: 10.4324/9781003160250-2

This chapter investigates the occupational identity and culture of chefs in commercial kitchen settings. In particular, the chapter explores the social structures and processes (i.e., the kitchen "ideology", symbols, rituals, rites, and myths) that help to perpetuate a sense of cohesion, identity, and belonging that defines "being a chef" (Cooper, 2012).

Occupational identity

Identity is an ambiguous and contested concept, which has been used differently across various social science disciplines and therefore generated a variety of meanings (Ashcraft, 2013), making any definition of the term a difficult task (Brubaker & Cooper, 2000). Sökefeld (1999) retraces the shift that the usage of the term "identity" has undergone within social sciences in the past few decades. As the Latin root of the term illustrates – *identitas*, from *idem*, "the same" – the original meaning of "identity" was "sameness" and in psychology this meant "selfsameness", that is, "a disposition of basic personality features acquired mostly during childhood and, once integrated, more or less fixed" (Sökefeld, 1999, p. 417). Drawing upon Erikson (1980), the awareness of having an identity thus meant being aware of one's own continuity and sameness, whilst being aware that others recognised such sameness and continuity.

Although it would be possible to continue at great length with a generic discussion of identity, our concern is with the realm of work and most specifically with the *occupational identity* of chefs and their brigades. In addition to the analytical categories of gender, ethnicity, class, sexuality, and age frequently used in academic definitions of individual identity, it seems legitimate to include a person's work/occupation as a significant contributor to identity, especially in light of the centrality of work to people's lives in industrialised societies (Van Maanen, 2010). Hughes (1971) argued that our work is directly linked to our sense of self, our course of being, and our way of life. In addition, Saunders (1981a, p. 128) has argued that "the question 'Who am I?' is increasingly seen by many social interpreters in an occupational sense". An examination of the relationship between work roles and identity is thus seen as an anchor point to the study of identity formation (Fraher & Gabriel, 2014). Cooper (2012) suggests that social thinkers have always, since the birth of sociology, shown some concern for the relationship between work and identity, albeit implicitly (Figure 2.1). In a post-WW2 context, the Symbolic Interactionist stance and its derivatives in occupational sociology posit the centrality of pre-defined occupational roles and reference groups to identity (i.e., Becker, 1963; Hughes, 1971; Goffman, 1959) and the interrelationship between the societal status conferred to a person's occupation and that person's self-image and sense of self-worth (Saunders, 1981a).

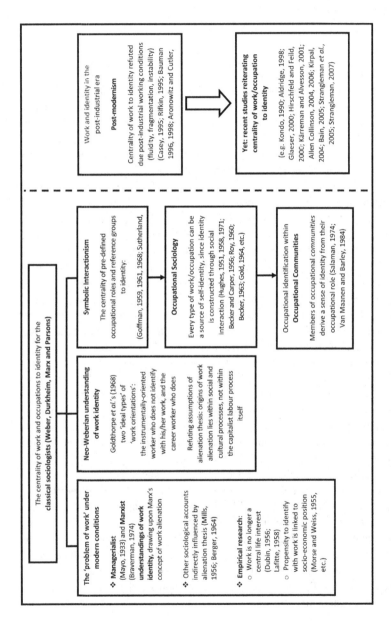

Figure 2.1 Theoretical approaches to work identity Source: Cooper (2012), p. 33

In response to criticisms directed at occupational sociology, studies of occupational communities do not generalise the applicability of the process of work identity formation to all types of work but instead focus on occupational identification within occupational *communities*, for which the defining criteria and determinants have been outlined in the work of Salaman (1986) and Van Maanen and Barley (1984). Whilst the study of chefs' occupational identity could benefit from an analysis of the occupation from the perspective of existing theories on occupational communities, the latter have ceased to be current objects of investigation for sociologists since the advent of the post-modern debate (i.e., Casey, 1995; Bauman, 1998; Beck, 2000).

Yet, despite the undeniable changes that have marked the world of work in the post-industrial era (fluidity, fragmentation, and instability), generalisations about the loss of identification with work are found wanting in the face of the enduring significance of work, and shared workplace cultures in particular, for many occupational groups (Strangleman, 2012). Based on the above discussion and the post-modern tradition, it would be therefore possible to suggest that a person's work/occupation is still a significant contributor to identity in modern society.

Occupational culture

Although there is little consensus in the work literature on what constitutes a *culture*, occupational cultures are often understood as "*those systems that develop in physically and socially separate work settings*" whereby "*members of ... [occupational] groups share a sense of common identity and perspective that transcends the place where they work*" (Rothman, 1998, p. 44). Organisational and occupational researchers have tended to focus on single and discrete elements of culture, such as rituals, symbols, and myths (e.g., Weick, 1979; Pfeffer, 1981; Martin, 1982), thus leading to the violation of traditional anthropological conceptions of culture (e.g., Kluckhohn, 1942) which stress how cultural elements closely interact with one another. Trice and Beyer (1984) argue that this lack of integration can be attributed to the fact that researchers often fail to place their chosen cultural concepts within some overall definition of occupational culture, therefore highlighting the need for better conceptualisation of the term. Based on a comprehensive review of the field, Trice and Beyer (1984) conclude that an occupational culture is made of two interdependent components: (1) its substance or the networks of meanings contained in its *ideologies*, that is, the beliefs, values, and norms of conduct that allow members of an occupation to make sense of the world in which they work; and (2) its *cultural forms* or the means by which an occupation conveys its ideologies to its

Figure 2.2 Occupational culture elements Source: adapted from Trice and Beyer
(1984) and Trice (1993)

members, such as rites, rituals, ceremonies, symbols, physical artefacts,
stories, and myths. In *Occupational Subcultures in the Workplace*, Trice
(1993) revisits the above arguments in more depth and explains that whilst
cultural forms are observable entities, ideologies are abstract and taken-
for-granted ideas, which help justify the ongoing behaviour of occupational
members and provide members with clear guidelines for action and social
interaction (Figure 2.2).

To illustrate his argument, Trice (1993, p. 41) cites the ideology of
prostitutes who believe that they serve important social functions by help-
ing to deter rapes and save troubled marriages and by providing com-
fort and sexual satisfaction (Bryan, 1966); and that of accountants who
believe that they reduce ignorance and generate consensus in organisations by means of rational knowledge and fact (Montagna, 1971). Aside
from beliefs, ideologies are often most clearly embodied in values, which
express "what is valuable or worthless, respected or disdained, important
or unimportant, commendable or deplorable" (Rothman, 1998, p. 53).
Thus, while journalists value the search for newsworthy events, scientists seek to push back the frontiers of knowledge, and sportsmen/women
advocate the confrontation of pain and injury under all circumstances
(Rothman, 1998).

Trice (1993) points out that occupational members can become very
emotionally attached to their ideologies, therefore leading to the emergence
of an ethnocentric ("us"-versus-"them") mentality and sometimes to social
isolation through a process of self-segregation (as in the case of jazz musi-
cians: see Becker, 1951), as other groups with different beliefs are distrusted
and disliked. Trice's conceptualisation offers a useful working model for
analysing occupational cultures, as it precludes researchers from examining
cultural forms in isolation from the group's underlying beliefs and values.
Based on Trice's (1993) work, in our discussion here we consider both the
occupational ideology of chefs and its associated cultural forms. It is also
argued that identity and culture are intertwined in the sense that the cultural

components of an occupational culture operate to reinforce a sense of identity amongst its occupational members.

Chefs' occupational identity and culture

The identity of chefs is, first and foremost, rooted in social interaction and derived from the socio-cultural practices of their occupational group (Bourdieu, 1990; Burkitt, 1994). Their occupational identity is formed through the dialectic of internal-external identification, as conceptualised by Jenkins (2004). Their identity is therefore influenced both by their occupational peer group, who constitute "significant others", and by the views and attitudes of "others" (non-chefs), towards them in the "outside world" (Cameron et al., 1999; Cooper et al., 2017; Goffman, 1959; Kang et al., 2010; Palmer et al., 2010; Saunders, 1981a). The outside world is the wider audience of society at large, all of whom look upon the world of chefs through the window provided by the media. In this respect, the media and the general public comprise the chefs' "generalised other" (Mead, 1934). Yet, chefs are also compelled to build a sense of identify by drawing from the existing meanings and ways of doing things that have informed and characterised the occupational culture of chefs for many generations (Berger & Luckmann, 1966; Bloisi & Hoel, 2008).

It is argued that individuals working in the same occupation develop distinctive occupational, *not* organisational, cultures (from which they derive common values and sets of behaviour) because of the amount of similarity in work and social settings (Gomez-Mejia, 1983; Paoline, 2003). Although the development of a shared workplace culture has often been linked to the process of work identity formation, as illustrated in the case of occupational communities (Barth, 1969), it is right to point out that the sharing of cultural features is not in itself sufficient for a group of individuals to develop a sense of identity: "Socially relevant factors alone become diagnostic for membership, not the overt "objective" differences" (ibid., p. 15). As both Barth (1969) and Cohen (1985) have suggested, once a group has negotiated its identity at the boundary with other groups, cultural traits may, however, become symbols of identity that help perpetuate a sense of belonging amongst the group members. Although occupational cultures are often acknowledged to form integral parts of organisational cultures, it is interesting to note, along with Hofstede et al. (1990) and Trice (1993), that occupational cultures have largely been overlooked by organisational cultures, researchers, and scholars.

The earliest systematic investigation of restaurant workers was Whyte's (1948) action-research study of restaurant and kitchen behaviour in a large Chicago restaurant, which is firmly rooted in the human relations tradition (Lewin, 1947). Nevertheless, as highlighted by Wood (1997), remarkably little methodical analysis of the work of chefs has been carried out until today. In the UK context, only the now-dated research of Chivers (1972, 1973) is dedicated entirely to the occupation of chefs and cooks, although Chivers's quantitative study predominantly focuses on occupational choice and expectations, and corresponding class consciousness, and thus does not directly deal with chefs' and cooks' occupational culture and identity. In the US context, a notable exception can be found in the work of Fine (1996a, 1996b), most of which is based on fieldwork carried out in the 1980s in four Minnesota restaurants (all in one city). Through participant observation, Fine systematically analyses the work of chefs and cooks from a sociological perspective and depicts how chefs use occupational rhetoric to describe themselves as scientists, artists, accountants, surgeons, psychiatrists, and handymen in a complex and malleable conceptualisation of their professional self. These bundles of rhetorical images were provisional, situationally dependent and, like self-constructed narratives, not necessarily consistent with each other (Fraher & Gabriel, 2014).

Furthermore, a number of studies have focused their attention on kitchen bullying and violence (Giousmpasoglou et al., 2018; Johns & Menzel, 1999), and its effects on hotel-organisation culture (Cameron et al., 1999). Similarly, Alexander et al. (2012) investigated the bullying behaviour experienced mostly by younger and junior in ranking chefs; they found bullying behaviour to be a cohesive aspect of the chefs' occupational culture that doesn't affect either job satisfaction or commitment. Burrow et al. (2015) provided an anecdotal account of a (male) chef's experiences from the early stages of his career as a *commis chef* to the day he got his first job as a head chef in an *haute cusine* restaurant. Alongside identity and culture, this empirical research demonstrates the occupational challenges and frustrations in a working environment that is described as "mundane, degrading and dehumanising" as well as "thrilling, exciting and rewarding" (ibid., p. 1).

The occupational culture in commercial kitchens is also characterised by low pay and worker exploitation on a global scale. Low pay was found to be responsible for a number of issues such as low productivity (Tongchaiprasita & Ariyabuddhiphongs, 2016), low employee satisfaction (Chuang et al., 2009), increased employee turnover (Pratten, 2003a), and employee burnout (Kang et al., 2010). A number of wage-theft cases with the involvement of celebrity chefs have been in the news occasionally in the past decade. In the UK, chef Michel Roux Jr paid kitchen staff well below the average minimum wage. In Australia, the latest celebrity chef-linked wage-theft scandal involved Heston Blumenthal's fine dining restaurant *Dinner by Heston* in Melbourne, allegedly underpaying its staff by A\$4 million (Schneiders & Millar, 2018). Other cases in Australia's hospitality industry worker exploitation include the former Masterchef judge George Calombaris (his company underpaying staff by $7.8 million), Shannon Bennett's Vue de monde restaurant (accused of forcing staff to work up to 30 hours of unpaid overtime each week), and Neil Perry's Rockpool Dining Group (accused of "audacious" time-sheet tampering potentially worth up to A$10 million in unpaid overtime) (Robinson & Brenner, 2020). In the US, celebrity chef Mario Batali has been sued twice, in 2010 and 2017, for paying restaurant workers under minimum wage, withholding staff tips, and unfair dismissals (Plagianos, 2017). Another case, of a not-so-publicised legal dispute, saw more than 150 of Geoffrey Zakarian's (TV chef and restauranteur) former employees taking him to court in a class-action lawsuit in 2011 (Fox, 2011). The restaurant staff exploitation (including kitchen staff – see Box 2.1) phenomenon is not exhausted on the above examples; these cases are indicative of the challenges related to people management in kitchen brigades.

BOX 2.1 WAGE EXPLOITATION IN CELEBRITY CHEF RESTAURANTS

The latest celebrity-chef-linked wage-theft scandal, with the high-end restaurant Dinner by Heston Blumenthal in Melbourne, allegedly underpaying its staff by A$4 million, is the tip of the iceberg for wage exploitation in the hospitality industry. Blumenthal joins a line of celebrity chefs linked to cases of million-dollar wage theft. There's former Masterchef judge George Calombaris's company underpaying staff by $7.8 million. There's Shannon Bennett's Vue de monde restaurant accused of forcing staff to work up to 30 hours of unpaid overtime each week. There's Neil Perry's Rockpool Dining Group, accused of "audacious" time-sheet tampering potentially worth up to $10 million in unpaid overtime. While the Rockpool claim has yet to be adjudicated by Australia's Fair Work Ombudsman, it did agree in October 2018 to back-pay staff $1.6 million. Perry told Fairfax Media Rockpool had made "a few changes" to better comply with the law. "It's always hard in restaurants", he said, "but I believe we would be one of very few, if any, that are complying with it currently".

Unpaid overtime

Dinner by Heston, which went into liquidation in December, allegedly underpaid staff by at least A$4 million over four years, according to the administrator's report leaked to the *New Daily*. The restaurant carries Blumenthal's name though he does not own it. Former Dinner by Heston chef William Trist told the *New Daily* he never worked fewer than 60 hours a week, and sometimes more than 80 hours. Our findings are in line with this and the other celebrity-linked cases mentioned above. Unpaid overtime is the most common form of wage theft. Many chefs and apprentices told us of working more than 20 hours of unpaid work a week during peak periods. Expectations of unpaid overtime were described to us as an intrinsic part of the hospitality business model. It wasn't a case of inadvertent compliance due to a complicated award system (as suggested by one-time MasterChef Australia judge Matt Moran). It was clear to both bosses and workers. One apprentice told us their employer justified it in the following terms: "We don't have the budget for it. So we need to wait until we have the budget and pay you."

Penalty rates and entitlements

The next most common form of wage theft, our research suggests, is not paying penalty rates. The majority of interviewees worked Sunday shifts or overtime or through breaks in exchange for the promise of time off, or accepted as compensation meals that might have been thrown away anyway. Our interviews also suggest underpayment of entitlements such as superannuation contributions is common. Younger workers in particular were often unaware their superannuation was not being paid correctly until it was too late. One factor contributing to this is the cash culture in the hospitality industry. As one apprentice told us:

> At my first job I asked them if I could be on the books and they said yes, but I didn't get any pay slips. When I left that job I asked my former manager if I have a superannuation account or something, and he said no.

Unpaid work trials

Unpaid work trials appear to be common too. Two young chefs told us about being duped by the same Sydney restaurant, being asked to work at least three days for free. Neither were offered a job. "Talking to my classmates", a culinary student said, "it's common doing free trials". One cultural tradition contributing to owners pulling this stunt is the "chef's sabbatical", when aspirational chefs do "stages", working for free in renowned restaurants to learn from esteemed chefs. A "stagiaire" may volunteer for up to six months to hone their craft and improve their career prospects. "I've done loads of stages", one chef told us. She travelled for months in the United States and Britain, working in the best restaurants for free. She accepted it was standard practice in the industry to build a career.

This toxic culture is contributing to workers quitting the industry. That's a problem for a sector facing a shortage of 59,500 chefs by 2023 compounded by rising traineeship incompletion rates.

Source: adapted from Robinson, R. and Brenner, M. (2020).
All these celebrity restaurant wage-theft scandals point to
an industry norm. Available at: https://theconversation.com/
all-these-celebrity-restaurant-wage-theft-scandals-point-
to-an-industry-norm-131286

Identity and culture creation in commercial kitchens

The process of chefs' identity creation and formation can be better understood by analysing the cultural aspects of this occupational group (Palmer et al., 2010). Cohen (1985) argues that "community" implies both the notion of similarity and that of difference, insofar as members of a group have something in common with each other, whilst the thing they have in common distinguishes them from the members of other possible groups. Drawing upon the work of Cohen (1985), it becomes clear that chefs derive a sense of belonging, loyalty, and similarity with their peers, by collectively constructing and embracing a front of similarity through shared symbols and other markers of identity which communicate what "being a chef" means (Burrow et al., 2015; Kang et al., 2010). Belonging is therefore established on the basis of a shared culture, as the following quote clearly illustrates:

The only friends I've got are in the industry, I've got no friends outside the industry, I've got nobody that's a painter, or this, or this, or this, I don't know anyone from where I grew up; all I know is chefs. If you look through my phone and my mobile, they're all chefs. Chefs or waiters – that's it – or suppliers. And you just think about it, and you think to yourself, "Why haven't I got any proper friends?" Proper friends wouldn't understand what I do." I can't have a f**king Saturday night off. … And to be honest with you, I wouldn't know what to talk about with them. I don't know what to talk to normal people about, because all I know is food.

(Cooper, 2012, p. 227)

Chefs are more than just a group of people; they are a group of people with something in common with each other which distinguishes them from other groups. In other words, they are a community of common-minded individuals. Bourdain (2000, p. 124) argues that chefs share a peculiar worldview, together with unusual customs, rituals, and practices that define them as a "tribe". Their unsocial working hours indeed contribute to their exclusion of "normal" social interaction and their subsequent deep commitment to their colleagues, or what Bourdain (2000, p. 56) refers to as a "blind, near-fanatical loyalty … under battlefield conditions".

Based on Douglas' (1982) theory of "grid/group" analysis, it can be argued that, taken as a whole, the occupational culture of chefs is characterised by a strong "group" identity and strong "grid" dimension characteristic of tight work-groups and communities – "wolves" in Mars's (1982) terms – whereby group boundaries are strongly defined. As the internal validating mechanisms highlighted clearly illustrate, membership of the chef community is based upon a shared understanding of the criteria for membership, in other words, they speak the same language. From the following quote, it is evident that having "done their time" and "earned their stripes" and the subsequent right to be called "chef", chefs share a common bond between them, a shared feeling of understanding, an affinity with one another, a sense of camaraderie, and a feeling of mutual respect:

When you hit this Michelin standard, then there's a respect there, I think. Once you get into the higher echelons of achieving, then, from other places of similar achievement, there seems to be a respect, I think. I wouldn't think twice about phoning just about anybody from a starred restaurant, or hotel, or whatever to speak to another chef. You've earned your stripes, I think. And you do get a respect from other chefs, definitely.

(Cooper, 2012, p. 224)

It is further evident that membership of the chef community is based on the ability to do the job. Chefs' induction and socialisation process is crucial for the new member's acceptance or rejection by the rest of the group. Cooper et al. (2017) argue that the cultural acceptance amongst chefs is global and transcends social class, gender, sexuality, and race/ethnicity.

Furthermore, it can be suggested, that the psychological boundaries of the chef community are constructed by the nature of the work and the routines and tasks associated with being a chef. The nature of the work defines the worldview, the value system of the chef community. On the other hand, the perception of the outside world with regard to the status and standing of the occupation and the image of chefs is neatly illustrated in the following quote:

> I think chefs are still pretty much lumped into the category – sort of fairly – of being hard, disciplined, pretty tyrannical, often abusive, leaders at the top of a long ladder that they have had to climb themselves being abused, and having to work like dogs all the way from the bottom of that long ladder.
>
> (Cooper, 2012, p. 290)

It is particularly interesting to note that despite the evident elevation of the status and standing of the occupation and the new-found respect and recognition afforded chefs themselves, the perception of the outside world with regard to the image of chefs is still somewhat spontaneously associated with the deeply ingrained archetypal cultural stereotype of the aggressive, authoritarian, tyrannical, temperamental, volatile, violent, and abusive chef (Cooper, 2012).

The literature identifies a few of the cultural symbols which denote chefs' belongingness and occupational enculturation, such as the quality and quantity of their (own) kitchen knives, their ability to chop rapidly and efficiently (Saunders, 1981a, 1981b; Fine, 1996b), and their knowledge of French service and French phrases (Bloisi & Hoel, 2008). Although no other symbols or rituals have been identified in the literature, the existence of kitchen stories has however been acknowledged, notably with reference to violence, bullying, and working long busy shifts (Johns & Menzel, 1999; Wood, 1997). The following quote confirms the existence of such culture in commercial kitchens:

> I've worked in kitchens where people have literally been stood on their section in tears, blokes crying. The sort of mental abuse and physical abuse that I've seen people take is really, really bad, especially in some of the more upmarket kitchens. However, I don't think that it is as rife as it was in the 90s. ... But you hear stories from people that worked in certain kitchens, and if you believe what you hear, then it's still pretty bad. But then there's some sort of sick pleasure that people get out of saying, "Oh, I worked here and he used to whip me every day, and he used to stick a knife in me," and all this carry on. For some reason, they like it.
>
> (Cooper, 2012, p. 298)

Conclusion

The discussion in this chapter regarding the occupational culture and identity in commercial kitchens suggests that the self-image of chefs and cooks is influenced by a number of factors. A significant component of the self-image of chefs is that they are engaged in a similar career path as compared to that which exists in the higher professions; chefs tend to compare the stages of their own careers to those of doctors and lawyers (Fine, 1996a, 1996b). The world of an individual employee in the restaurant industry is a very closed and incestuous one (Kang et al., 2010). Chefs' friendship groups only tend to contain other chefs and frequent movement between kitchens is commonplace. As a direct consequence, the occupational community of chefs is much more close-knit than is seen in other professions (Palmer et al., 2010). Chefs are solely judged by their peers on their ability to do the job. The findings of this study suggest also that the kitchen is a meritocracy, irrespective of social class, gender, sexuality, and race/ethnicity (Fine, 1987). A kitchen brigade is often compared to a family and engenders a high degree of group solidarity, bonding, and camaraderie between its members (Trice, 1993). This is what informs the unusually tight-knit and what is often seen by outsiders as walled-off nature of the restaurant industry. Part of the social cost of membership of this family is the demonstration of dedication to the familial group (Cohen, 1985). This cost is paid through the individual putting the needs of the group above their own, in the sense that they will not take time off for sickness and they will work through pain or injury (Burrow et al., 2015). Indeed, the burns, scalds, cuts, and scars attained whilst working in the kitchen are seen as signifiers of occupational validity (Bourdain, 2000; Simpson, 2006; White, 1990).

Furthermore, the perception of the outside world with regard to the image of chefs is still somewhat spontaneously associated with the deeply ingrained archetypal cultural stereotype of the aggressive, authoritarian, tyrannical, temperamental, volatile, violent, and abusive chef (Bloisi & Hoel, 2008; Cooper, 2012). It was identified that the aggressive and violent nature of induction into the catering industry for young, new recruits is the result of imitation on the part of more senior, higher ranking chefs – these chefs in turn imitating the behaviour learnt from and handed down by their superiors during their time as new recruits (Salin & Hoel, 2011). Indeed, however disastrous the consequences, it can therefore be argued that from a cultural viewpoint chefs are able to derive a sense of identity by embracing and perpetuating the myth of the creative and violent chef. The myth is further reinforced by the fact that the chefs who make it to the top of the profession are often the ones who have willingly endured harsh working conditions and mistreatment (Johns & Menzel, 1999). It was revealed that this violent and aggressive means of socialisation in commercial kitchens is often regarded as being analogous with the means of induction to the military and paramilitary organisations (i.e., police and fire service) (Alexander et al., 2012).

3 People management and leadership in commercial kitchens

Introduction

This chapter investigates the functions of people management and leadership in the context of commercial kitchens. For almost two centuries management and leadership in commercial kitchens has been based upon the Brigades system and the principles established by Auguste Escoffier in the 19th century. This regimental system survived until today and is observed even in contemporary kitchen settings and high-performing teams. The chapter identifies the key people management challenges in commercial kitchens and proposes best practices to motivate, engage, and retain talented chefs and kitchen professionals in commercial kitchens globally.

DOI: 10.4324/9781003160250-3

Introduction to Human Resources Management

Human Resources Management (HRM) is the strategic approach of managing people in organisations in an effective and efficient manner. HRM is the main vehicle for service organisations to achieve competitive advantage and maximise employee performance through policies and systems. Human Resources (HR) departments are responsible for employee benefits, recruitment, training and development, appraisals, rewards, and the implementation of employment-related legislation (Armstrong, 2009).

Various definitions are provided such as the one from Armstrong (2016, p. 7) who defines HRM as "a strategic, integrated and coherent approach to the employment, development and well-being of the people working in organisations"; and Boxall and Purcell (2016, p. 7) who define HRM as "the process through which management builds the workforce and tries to create the human performances that the organisation needs".

The key HR functions in commercial kitchen settings are depicted in Figure 3.1. The HRM cycle begins with HR planning. This initial stage refers to the process of people forecasting. It involves the investigation and analysis of demand and supply of labour force, job analysis, and forecasting for the organisation with some costing included. Next is Recruitment and Selection; at this point having identified the people needed, the organisation aims to attract applicants to match certain job criteria. Filtration is done through the selection process in order to short list candidates for interviews. Once people are selected the final decision is made and hiring takes place (Armstrong, 2009, 2016). Onboarding is the key process as described in the section "Onboarding" of this chapter. Induction used to take place to familiarise new recruits with the company, however nowadays the first three months are found to be vital for retaining people. Onboarding provides new recruits with information, practices, policies, communication with other colleagues, and in general familiarisation with all aspects of the business which is actually monitored. Training and Development are also important to provide opportunities to existing employees to progress in the company and develop further skills. Motivation, Reward, and Performance Management are also part of the HRM cycle. Regular performance appraisals take place which relate to reward, incentives, staff motivation, and decisions on required staff training. Grievances and Disciplinary Action are also a responsibility of the HR department. Employee relations are considered in this case, with a focus on Health and Safety, Conflict Management, Work-life Balance, and Counselling. Finally, Organisational Exit is when the employment relationship ends voluntarily or involuntarily (i.e., end of career, retirement, redundancy, etc.). All these processes are integral to the success of organisations especially for commercial kitchens due to the culture, the context, and the working conditions

Figure 3.1 The key HRM functions in commercial kitchen settings

as further discussed. No single process can work in isolation, as conformity and cohesiveness are important for HR strategy success (Armstrong, 2016).

A key objective of the HR department is to implement practices that are strategically designed, aiming to attract and maintain an effective workforce and retain talent. Organisations consider HRM as an extra cost (Wang et al., 2011), ignoring the need for proper and effective human resources practices and implementation of these practices to business. Nowadays, an increasing number of foodservice businesses recognise the importance of HRM, the issues of managing people in the industry as well as the challenges of finding and retaining good employees. Studies propose that HRM practices contribute to improved turnover (Murphy & Olsen, 2008), labour productivity (Lin et al., 2011), asset and equity return, and profit margin (Kim & Kim, 2005).

Research on the chef's occupation started almost at the same time the media started presenting Michelin-starred chefs such as Alain Ducasse, Gordon Ramsey, and Heston Blumenthal, among others. Various aspects of the chef's occupation and culture have been researched, i.e., work on kitchen violence and bullying (Cooper et al., 2017; Bloisi & Hoel, 2008), occupational stress (Murray-Gibbons & Gibbons, 2007), retention and training (Robinson & Beesley, 2010), liberal education (Magnusson Sporre et al., 2015), and gender (Harris & Giuffre, 2015). Research on head chefs and HRM practices remains rare (Allen & Mac Con Iomaire, 2017).

Challenges of managing human resources in commercial kitchens

Human resources managers, especially within the foodservice industry, are currently facing some major issues. The major concern has been the lack of skills and labour shortages over the past five years, which worsened with the COVID 19 pandemic. People1st (2017) reports that 22% of vacancies in UK hospitality were for chefs. Between 2012 and 2017 the number of posted vacancies for sous chef roles increased by 64% and for head chef roles by 33% (p. 6). The chef shortage is not unique to the UK, many countries are affected as well. Similar chef shortages are reported in Europe, North America, and Australia (see also Chapter 9). People1st (2017, p. 12) identify six main factors which contribute to the chef shortage:

1. Increased demand for chefs;
2. The changing nature of chef roles;
3. A shrinking labour pool (unemployment, changing demographics, attracting and retaining female chefs);
4. A small number of chef apprentices entering the sector;
5. Few full-time chef students entering and staying in the sector;
6. The changing nature of chef turnover and chefs leaving the profession (2017, p. 12).

Robinson and Barron (2007) identified recruitment problems as an underlying factor for challenges in HRM in commercial kitchens. Staff turnover and mobility have always been an issue in the sector. Most research on mobility emanates from broader studies and conclusions from multi-occupational and multi-organisational samples have little relevance to commercial kitchens. Robinson and Barron (2007, p. 915) continue with an argument that "turnover behaviour is situational and as such a 'mono-occupational' focus is embraced". Occupational culture differs across the hospitality industry sectors, as chefs for example in hotels are more ambitious, whereas in restaurants they are professionals, artists, businessmen, or labourers. Hence, chefs' turnover, mobility, and skills should be examined from an occupational standpoint, which has been ignored by research (Marinakou & Giousmpasoglou, 2020; Robinson & Barron, 2007). Another issue has been the changing demographics of the labour force in the foodservice industry. The commercial kitchen sector has historically relied heavily on young people to fill positions, but the decreasing number of new entrants to the labour market has changed the profile of workers, as it relies mainly on migrants (Marinakou & Giousmpasoglou, 2020). Evidently, chefs should build cross-cultural skills to be able to manage people in their kitchens. Strategic HRM requires chefs to demonstrate sophisticated talent management, with a focus on people-handling, technological proficiency, and leadership skills (Marinakou & Giousmpasoglou, 2019).

As discussed in Chapters 2, 7, and 8, chefs' occupational culture in commercial kitchens poses some unique challenges. The media interest in abusive behaviour in kitchens has led to research in this field. Abuse has been shown as a necessary part of the job; for example, the British chef Gordon Ramsay in the *Hell's Kitchen* television programme is portrayed as being abusive, although in his biography he clearly demonstrates examples of his staff loyalty (Bloisi & Hoel, 2008). Others claim that abuse is part of the socialisation process that teaches young cooks how to function in the kitchen and become harder (Bourdain, 2004). Other challenges of working in kitchens include prevailing cultural norms and organisational policies relating to bullying, emotional abuse, sexual harassment, commitment to long hours demanded by management, authoritarian and hierarchical management style, power based on position, plus employees starting from the bottom and working up. Moreover, seasonality, unpredictable economic climates, poor working conditions, low pay, stereotypes, and the repetitive and unchallenging character of chefs' work are relevant occupational challenges. In this demanding environment staff motivation is vital. The study of individual behaviour and group dynamics, plus organisational behaviour in commercial kitchens, is critical for practitioners.

Job satisfaction benefits organisations as it has been found to negatively correlate with work stress, absenteeism, and voluntary turnover intention and to positively correlate with employee performance, productivity, and job involvement (Huang, 2006). Work stress is common among kitchen staff. Major sources of work stress include job demands and characteristics, individual characteristics and expectations, and organisational characteristics and processes. Organisational factors including rotation, pay inequalities, poor communication, lack of training, noise, excessive heat or cold, safety hazards, time pressures, and overload contribute to work stress (Bloisi & Hoel, 2008). People in commercial kitchens work under a lot of pressure with intense deadlines. The environment is usually filled with heat, smoke, humidity, and worsening working conditions. Bindu and Reddy (2013) add that the harsh work environment, injuries, and illnesses impact chefs' lives, income, and families. In their study they discuss the quality of the air, lighting, noise, heat, and cleanliness which also cause stress to staff in commercial kitchens. Studies propose that turnover intention is correlated with work dissatisfaction, different personal characteristics, and work stress (Huang, 2006). All these challenging conditions in the kitchen affect kitchen staff attitudes and the quality of their work. The climate of excellent service leads to favourable customer outcomes. To achieve this, mechanisms should be in place such as effective recruitment, staff motivation, compensation, teamwork building, and leadership as they are discussed in this chapter.

People management

Restaurants are struggling to manage labour costs and to recruit and retain talent, especially for kitchens. They are looking for new ways to solve problems through employee motivation, incentives, and empowerment. It is vital to provide chefs and cooks with all the required resources, tools, and equipment to perform their tasks. Kitchen staff should be knowledgeable; hence hiring quality kitchen staff should be a priority (Marinakou & Giousmpasoglou, 2020).

Recruitment and selection

Political changes have contributed to the recruitment of chefs. For example, Brexit has posed restrictions on EU workers going into the UK. Other countries rely on immigrants to work in the sector (i.e., Australia, New Zealand, and the Netherlands). In commercial kitchens job hopping is common and sometimes a good sign. Kitchen staff move around in order to gain experience (Wellton et al., 2019). Those with reliable track records and relevant experience should be on top of the hiring list. The right attitude and eagerness to learn are important. The right employees complement the organisational culture and positively impact the customer service experience. The right employees with the right attitude, skills, knowledge, and abilities will adapt and embrace the business culture, values, and mission (Marinakou & Giousmpasoglou, 2020). Poor recruitment processes have negative effects on business performance. If people in the kitchen are not the right fit then they will more likely leave early resulting in high staff turnover (Allen & Mac Con Iomaire, 2017). High staff turnover is expensive and results in increased costs for rehiring, for training, poor team morale, and low productivity. Martin (2004) suggested that team cohesion and the nature of the job itself explain job satisfaction among staff in kitchens; in order to maintain cohesion abuse is accepted. Recognition of important characteristics and competencies (see Chapter 5) to identify suitable candidates for recruitment contributes to remaining competitive.

Onboarding

The onboarding process is also known as induction training, when the HR used to have a day of orientation to familiarise new employees with the company's culture, standards, and policies (Bradt, 2015). High-performance companies use a more strategic process called "onboarding". Onboarding is the procedure of acculturating and integrating new employees into the business providing them with the tools and data to get creative. This process is adapted to the company and its needs, as new hires continue to receive training during onboarding which usually lasts three months. The length varies depending on the size of the organisation, the requirements of the job, and the employee's characteristics and experience. Onboarding is the second of four steps of an employee lifecycle (Booz et al., 2018, p. 2). Firstly, as part of the HRM process, onboarding starts by forecasting and HR planning in order to find the right talent. After recruitment it is about holding onto workers once they are on board (Talent Management, 2018). Once people pass through the onboarding process and the probation period, talent management takes place with training, development, and other incentives and processes in order to retain talent, which is important in commercial kitchens because staff turnover is high (Figure 3.2).

Onboarding software is available and is found to advance the retention of employees by 25%, reducing the high cost of turnover (Van Beek, 2020). For example, there are systems whereby 30 days before joining the organisation people are sent a welcome message, and then when they join, all facilities, IT, workspace, and equipment are ready, saving valuable time. A schedule is also sent with all pre-joining paperwork, such as policies and medical information.

Various tips are offered for successful onboarding as there is not much research available on the topic, especially for employees in commercial

Figure 3.2 Onboarding and talent retention

kitchens (Van Beek, 2020). Such tips include advice such as communicating with the new employee before the first working day. A one-day induction is not sufficient, but a proper timeframe should be established to allow time for reflection. HR managers should ensure "people and culture" are part of the programme and include information about non-negotiable behaviours. A member of the staff who specialises in engaging others could perform the role that focuses on staff integration and retention.

Staff motivation

Motivation is an inner drive that directs people "toward the satisfaction of certain needs and expectations" (Mullins, 1992) and helps explain why individuals behave in the way they do (Cullen, 2001). Chuang et al. propose that motivation can be studied either with a content approach focusing on people's needs/wants from the job or a process approach which explores the reasons why people behave the way they do (2009, p. 326). The role of head chefs is to create an environment where people can enjoy their work, hence they must have motivational skills to encourage people to work together and resolve conflicts (Amer, 2005). Head chefs should be able to motivate themselves as well, in order to be able to motivate others and have a sense of self-efficacy (Zopiatis, 2010).

Motivation factors are split into intrinsic and extrinsic; intrinsic motivators are those that satisfy people's psychological needs, achievement, advancement, and other values, and extrinsic motivators are those related to work conditions and other external factors that impact staff motivation and job satisfaction (Chuang et al., 2009). Studies propose that extrinsic factors are more important to motivate employees in hospitality (Lam et al., 2001; Smith et al., 1996). Others propose that extrinsic factors do not guarantee job satisfaction (Wong& Heng, 1999), but claim that staff motivation depends on employment status (i.e., seasonal or full-time), demographic background, and type of business amongst others. In such complex and demanding working conditions of commercial kitchens, it is vital to give credit and praise to people in front of others, showing respect to their work and effort. People are motivated by leaders who recognise and show appreciation for their work. All this helps in team building as well. Studies propose that successful restaurants are those where employees are creative and have fun and a joyful atmosphere reduces abuse in the workplace (Wellton et al., 2019). These restaurants are usually led by creative chefs, who motivate their team members and energise their staff reducing the costs associated with labour turnover. Training of chefs' apprenticeships on the socio-cultural world of haute cuisine should be done through the head chef's creativity, making the kitchen a situated learning environment for apprentices (Stierand, 2015). Michelin-starred chefs demonstrate top-down management styles as they believe that their kitchen staff are not experienced enough to develop new products and failure could damage the reputation of their restaurants. Nowadays, head chefs support their staff, train them and lead teamwork striving for excellence with constant supervision and micromanagement (Marinakou & Giousmpasoglou, 2020; Lane, 2014; Zopiatis, 2010). In order to motivate people, head chefs should create a kitchen with practices and work that give meaning to employees. The boring and repetitive content of kitchen work creates dissatisfaction and impacts well-being on the job (Wellton et al., 2019). Head chefs modernise organisational structures to ensure that young employees stay in the business (Lane, 2014).

Similarly, head chefs state that they continually learn from colleagues and that they can never be fully trained in their profession (Wellton et al., 2019). Korica et al. (2015) suggest that chefs bring their knowledge and skills in the kitchen and sharing these contributes to developing and/or altering practices. This creates meaning in a job that is routinised with low wages and motivates people to remain in the industry. Making people part of the decision making around food, menus, and working orders is a motivating factor in commercial kitchens (Figure 3.3). Chefs themselves need to be motivated, hence they need recognition of their work. Certificates of merit and appreciation, incentive programmes, promotion

Figure 3.3 Kitchen staff motivation tips. Source: adapted from Burton, L. (2017). How to foster motivation in your restaurant employees. Retrieved from: https://www.highspeedtraining .co.uk/hub/motivating-restaurant-staff/

opportunities, and support are some examples of motivational factors (Marinakou & Giousmpasoglou, 2020; Zopiatis, 2010; Chuang et al., 2009). The role of having a mentor is also found to motivate people in commercial kitchens. Having a mentor results in job involvement, higher organisational commitment, and increased job satisfaction (Allen & Mac Con Iomaire, 2017).

Teamwork

For successful service, people working in the kitchen must work together, collaborate, and cooperate. For example, if one person is off the staff morale may reduce. Tempers can run high as kitchen staff can be filled with adrenaline. Wellton et al. (2019, p. 402) state that "the organisational order in restaurant kitchens is teamwork, which is essential to achieve the lateral coordination needed to combine many different work processes related to different types of food preparation". Harris and Giuffre (2015, p. 88) depict the teamwork dynamics in commercial kitchens in the following example:

> Chelsea, a culinary instructor, describes these pressures: You're all about getting it done as perfect and as fast as you possibly can. You're constantly coming in trying to race the clock, get your station set up, and then boom, you're in service. It is intense. Waiters are coming in and asking for things. Nobody's happy. Nothing is right. There's fire. There's knives. Everything's going very quickly and moving around. Your mind is going a million miles a minute. So, somebody screws that up, then you are going to start whaling on them (laughs). You know what I mean? It's very important that that group be in a good dynamic. If they're not, then the whole thing just kind of falls apart. Everything you've all worked for that night is demolished because one person … so it's this teamwork kind of thing.

Teamwork is essential in dealing with all the challenges in the demanding context of professional kitchens. Nevertheless, it is also a competitive environment where all cooks are trying to move up to more prestigious cooking stations or even to positions such as sous chef. Extensive training of knowledge and teamwork building skills is crucial for high employee commitment in restaurants (Balazs, 2001). It is easy to find skilled cooks but hard to find those who have the mentality of working in teams or to train them in thinking, creativity, and sustainability.

Despite the hard working conditions and the fact that everyone in the kitchen concentrates on their tasks, the ambience is friendly. Lane (2014) proposed that teamwork is the success factor in restaurants. In a busy kitchen, there are many staff working in cramped spaces, with hot dishes, and many contributing to plating up plates of food with the utmost precision so as to avoid collisions. In their study, Bloisi and Hoel (2008) proposed that members of the team that act annoyingly are excluded from the team, as no excuse for such behaviour is given in traditional hierarchical kitchens.

Leadership

Leadership for head chefs is acquired through experience and management is not what they thought they would be doing when starting their career. Roosipöld and Longma (2014) claim that the compromise between being a professional chef and a leader is seldom part of the self-image of the head chefs. There are different styles of leadership found in commercial kitchens. Studies propose that chefs' leadership style impacts employees' job satisfaction and organisational performance (Marinakou & Giousmpasoglou, 2020; Zopiatis, 2010). The unfavourable economic conditions, fierce competition, and the nature of the restaurant industry have forced chefs to adopt methods and leadership styles that will help them achieve organisational goals, improve employee performance, and maintain quality of service (Marinakou & Giousmpasoglou, 2020). The pandemic has forced leaders in commercial kitchens to become agile and more adaptive problem-solvers and develop coaching skills. Coaching is a journey where the leader ensures the team members are committed to achieving goals and take responsibility and ownership of the outcome. Leaders in this case should be neutral and unbiased, especially when giving advice (Van Beek, 2020).

Although the way chefs manage and lead their kitchens could be used as a great example for other contexts, there is little research on leadership styles of chefs to provide more evidence (Delekovcan, 2013). One explanation could be that the unique characteristics of work in kitchens could not be transferred to other industries or business. As already presented in previous chapters, commercial kitchens are a dynamic environment, labour-intensive, where leading people is difficult. The best way to manage people in professional kitchens is to lead by example. For example, in their study Marinakou and Giousmpasoglou (2020) state that one chef said that if you leave your phone down the others will follow, hence chefs act and lead by example. Understanding the needs of staff in commercial kitchens may decrease the cost of recruitment, hiring, training, and turnover.

Most studies do not provide adequate data and evidence to support a specific leadership style and its effectiveness in commercial kitchens. For example, Balazs (2001) concentrated on three-starred Michelin chefs in France. His study presented a narrative on leadership rather than ways to succeed. There are many definitions of leadership. Northhouse (2010) suggested that leadership in organisations is about influencing and supporting team members to maintain the competitive advantage and sustain profitability. He proposed four main components of leadership: leadership is a process, leadership involves influence, leadership occurs in groups, and leadership involves common goals (Northouse, 2010, pp. 3–4). In their study, Marinakou and Giousmpasoglou (2020) and Zopiatis (2010) propose different competencies for chefs. In general, they propose that head chefs take various roles such as the leader, creator, and businessperson all at the same time. The main challenge they face is managing human resources as discussed previously. Interestingly, most chefs are not adequately trained to manage people (Allen & Mac Con Iomaire, 2017) and in general they develop leadership skills by experience (Marinakou & Giousmpasoglou, 2020). The tight budgets in restaurants do not provide opportunities for leadership training and developing, which in some cases may result in survival issues.

Kitchens are split in two, time with busy service hours and hours outside service. Lützen (2010, p. 72) describes service periods as "the process of making a product, that allows no flaws or errors, neither in production, timing of the production or in the delivery of the product while having a very perishable time periods". She further describes that during service periods, head chefs "need to be in charge of controlling quality, when to do what, taking the fast decisions, communicating everything in short precise messages and to secure the flow of the service". In non-service hours, according to Lützen (2010, p. 72) "not much leading appears to be necessary, unless technical question on e.g., cutting size, length of boiling, density etc. questions that the sous-chef just as often answers and instructs". Therefore, the context where leadership is exhibited along with organisational culture affect the leadership style to be adopted by chefs. The culture of commercial kitchens is described as a no-error culture, putting a lot of pressure on chefs.

Studies propose that chefs demonstrate directive leadership during non-service hours and give achievement-oriented and directive leadership during busy service hours (Delekovcan, 2013). Directive leaders are authoritative, use strict direction and command, close supervision, and set clear rules and high standards (Northouse, 2010). Achievement-oriented leaders motivate their team members to perform at the highest level, set challenging goals, and have high standards of excellence (Northouse, 2010).

Furthermore, Marinakou and Giousmpasoglou (2020) propose that head chefs should be flexible and open-minded. They should trust and empower their subordinates to perform their tasks and take initiatives. This is difficult for chefs who must give up control in this case and become role models. Particularly good communication skills are the key to encourage people and create a trusting environment, nurturing with support and care of human needs and well-being. In their study, Marinakou and Giousmpasoglou (2020) found that kitchen staff would like chefs to act as mentors and share their knowledge and experience. Great chefs practice mentorship, teach their teams, and emulate the skills and experience they have accumulated over the years. Studies propose that head chefs mentor their sous chef(s) in skills such as leading teams, effective communications, and dealing with high-stress workplaces (Marinakou & Giousmpasoglou, 2019; Zopiatis, 2010). Chefs also share the credit and praise their teams; these are all characteristics and leadership behaviours associated with transformational leadership which is found to be effective in the services context (Marinakou, 2019).

Leadership is less an actual individual competency such as a combination of determination, purposefulness, and performance contributing to an overarching strategic plan, but rather a "subtle, textured, complex embodied and highly situated mindset" (Carroll et al., 2008, p. 365). In commercial kitchens, proficiency in cooking requires disciplined hard work; hence day-to-day leadership activities such as decision making may be considered a routine rather than a leadership trait. Leadership in commercial kitchens applied by head chefs focuses on ensuring that the job is efficiently and effectively done (Allen & Mac Con Iomaire, 2017). In their study a head chef stated that "an ideal leader is a head chef who, although possibly hierarchical in leadership style, could optimise all the talents and competencies exhibited by the subordinates" (p. 416).

Emotional intelligence (EI) is found to be a success factor for chefs (Marinakou & Giousmpasoglou, 2020; Zopiatis, 2010). EI is about considering an employee's need and concerns as well as facing one's own limitations. In this case leaders should demonstrate their understanding of the situation, i.e., the impact of COVID-19 in order to gain their team's trust and commitment. Such leaders exhibit integrity and embrace the strengths of the organisation to find creative solutions. They are open to solutions for managing people, communicating with staff and stakeholders, and much more.

The discussion on leadership in a commercial kitchen context is summarised in Figure 3.4.

Conclusion

In order to attract and retain staff in commercial kitchens, changes in working conditions must occur. An understanding of the daily work is vital in order to motivate people and encourage them to remain in the foodservice industry. Daily work activities in commercial kitchens affect employees' motivation,

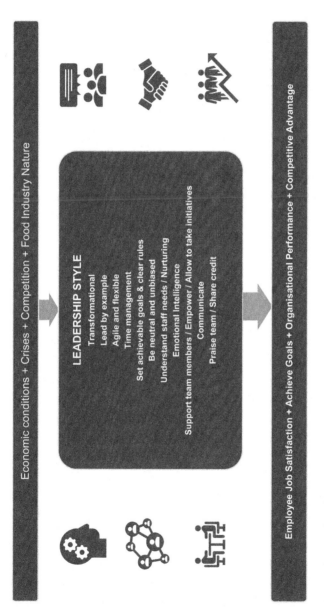

Figure 3.4 Leadership style in commercial kitchens

job satisfaction, and chef's leadership style. Effective and efficient HRM is vital for gaining a competitive advantage through human resources. Staff and managers-leaders in commercial kitchens are challenged by many factors, either organisational and/or occupational. Occupational rhetoric is part of the motivation and leadership process in this context. Chefs lead their teams by words and actions through activities of everyday work, being constantly present rather than being tied to an office. Chefs are agile and adapt their leadership style to the context, the size of the organisation and the brigade, and the changing situations. They demonstrate personal qualities that help them manage and lead their teams effectively.

4 Education and training for chefs

Introduction

Responding to the unprecedented growth of relevant professions, culinary education and training has recently claimed the spotlight. From its humble beginnings as an obscure discipline mostly associated with the vocational apprenticeship system, to its current "celebritised" status, culinary education – at all levels – is bestowed the task of adequately preparing the next generation of industry professionals. Nevertheless, and despite its long history, well-documented progress, and more recent popularity, culinary education is still in search of an identity. Challenges associated with the vocational versus academic nature of the educational offering, the scarcity

DOI: 10.4324/9781003160250-4

of culinary-specific quality indicators, and the disparity between technical and liberal arts courses create worrisome conceptual ambiguities, thus
necessitating the full attention of industry stakeholders. To help clarify the
situation, this chapter provides the concerned reader a realistic overview of
the status of culinary training and education, with specific emphasis on the
aforementioned challenges.

Culinary education: a historical perspective

Gastronomy (derived from the Greek word "Γαστρονομία"), the rules of
eating, can be traced back to Ancient Greece. Evidence suggests that the
term was first used by Archestratus (4th century BC) in his book (writ-
ings) describing culinary practices in the Mediterranean region (Wilkins
& Hill, 1994), whereas other ancient transcripts and artefacts suggest that
gastronomy evolved in areas extending from the Middle East all the way to
Asia. Despite the plethora of evidence as to the origins and development of
gastronomy in different regions of the world, which reveal interesting but
sometimes conflicting evidence (see for example the work of Kiefer, 2002),
there is a scarcity of information regarding formal culinary arts training.

Closely associated with the apprenticeship system – training under the
authority of an experienced (master) chef in order to gain the necessary
skills and experience – and the evolution of the craft guilds (the prede-
cessor to labour unions), vocational culinary training was gradually introduced over the course of the Middle Ages. According to Keller (1948),
young apprentices were "bound" to their master for a fixed period at the
latter's expense, and, in return, they had to comply with certain house rules,
which were historically acknowledged as authoritarian, abusive, brutal, and
aggressive (Parker, 2006). Over time, by putting in hard work and gaining
experience, these apprentices were promoted to journeymen whose rights
were protected by the guilds (Miles, 2007). As a result of these national
apprenticeship systems, guilds became the focal point in the provision of
vocational culinary training; a role which only began to fade with the industrial revolution.

The first cookbook – *Opera Dell'arte del Cucinare* – was developed
in 1570 by Bartolomeo Scappi, an Italian Renaissance chef who served
under three different Popes (Krohn, 2015). Scappi's book, divided into six
chapters, includes more than 1,000 recipes and 28 illustrations portraying
kitchen utensils of the era. Next, Francois Pierre La Varenne's *Le Cuisinier
Francais* (1651) is credited for instigating the transformation from medieval
to modern cooking, and in essence advancing French gastronomy into the
modern era; an era influenced by the work of some of the most influential
chefs in history, namely François Vatel (1631–1671) and Antoine Carême

(1784–1833), both known for serving aristocrats and royalty with extravagant gastronomic experiences (Kelly, 2004) (Figure 4.1).

The industrial revolution caused dramatic changes to culinary practices and professions alike, which already enjoyed both popularity and prestige, especially amongst the aristocracy. Chefs began to shift their focus to demonstrate their skills via more structured techniques and practices. Espousing this new paradigm, Auguste Escoffier (1846–1935), for many the most influential chef of the 20th century, introduced the hierarchical labour system; also known as the "partie" or the "brigade" system. This new approach revolutionised the culinary workplace, providing a structured approach that is even today considered ideal for education, career development, and on-the-job training (Gillespie, 1994). Gillespie added (p. 20):

> The partie system has always provided the means of sensitizing, stimulating, training and developing individuals to the stage where a thorough grounding and eventual specialism in the craft of the chef could be codified. To some, Escoffier's regime was viewed as a bureaucratically founded phenomenon constraining innovation in cuisine. However, the consequences of the partie system for chefs was that it created a formal career structure and spawned a culinary aristocracy comprising those who had made it through the hierarchy to become chefs de cuisine. The partie system was and remains a means of managing the division of labour in hotel and restaurant kitchens providing developmental stages of packages of skills which have to be mastered as a requirement for promotion, while supplying the employer with a mechanism for breaking up the division of labour into more calculable units, thus allowing tighter financial and human resource controls.

Finally, it is important to note Escoffier's immense contribution with the publication of his seminal cookbook *Le Guide Culinaire* (first published in French in 1903), for many the foundation of modern culinary arts (James, 2002) (Figure 4.2).

In Europe, the transformation of French cuisine from medieval to modern over the course of the 17th and 18th centuries was the driving force in the development of culinary education (Brown, 2005), which at the time was closely associated with the established apprenticeship system. This system, which enabled the transfer of cooking fundamentals from the experienced master chef to the apprentice, was later replaced by a more institutionalised and formal vocational approach (Emms, 2005). According to Trubek (2000), early specialised programmes aimed at enhancing students' practical food production skills and providing them with basic knowledge around safely using specialised equipment. Notable examples of institutions

OPERA DI M.
BARTOLOMEO
SCAPPI, CVOCO SECRETO
DI PAPA PIO V.

DIVISA IN SEI LIBRI,

Nel primo si cōtiene il ragionamēto che fa l'autore con Gio. suo discepolo.

Nel secondo si tratta di diuerse uiuande di carne sì di quadrupedi, come di uolatili.

Nel terzo si parla della statura, e stagione de pesci.

Nel quarto si mostrano le liste del presentar le uiuande in tauola cosi di grasso come di magro.

Nel quinto si contiene l'ordine di far diuerse sorti di paste, & altri lauori.

Nel sesto, & ultimo libro si ragiona de conualescenti, & molte altre sorti di uiuande per gli infermi.

Con il discorso funerale che fu fatto nelle esequie di Papa Paulo III.

Con le figure che fanno bisogno nella cucina, & alli Reuerendissimi nel Conclaue.

Col priuilegio del sommo Pontefice Papa Pio V. & dell' Illustrissimo Senato Veneto per anni XX.

Figure 4.1 Opera Dell'arte del Cucinare was developed in 1570 by Bartolomeo Scappi. Source: https://upload.wikimedia.org/wikipedia/commons/a/aa/ Scappi_Opera.jpg

 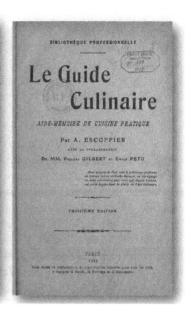

Figure 4.2 Images of Auguste Escoffier (1846-1935) and his seminal cookbook Le Guide Culinaire. Sources: https://en.wikipedia.org/wiki/Auguste _Escoffier#/media/File:Auguste_Escoffier_01.jpg & https://gallica.bnf .fr/ark:/12148/bpt6k96923116.texteImage

offering such specialised training included L'École Professionnelle de Cuisine et des Sciences Alimentaires which was established in 1883 by Charles Driessens, the Lausanne Hotel School founded in 1893 by hotelier Jacques Tschumi, and L'École de Cuisine du Cordon Bleu opened in Paris by Henri-Paul Pellaprat in 1895.

Culinary evolution in the US

In the US, the culinary scene was heavily influenced by 19th century migration, during which many European chefs decided to pursue a better life in the land of opportunities. Mostly seeking greater economic opportunities, renowned European chefs utilised their expertise to help shape the food culture of the American melting pot. Notable names include Charles Ranhofer, the chef at Delmonico's, the famous restaurant in New York, and author of *The Epicurean*, a cookbook published in 1894, and Antoine Alciatore, a French chef who immensely influenced Louisiana's creole cuisine. The transformation of the culinary culture in the US over the course of the 19th century provided the impetus for the development of relevant vocational education in the country.

With roots going back to 1879, the Boston Cooking School, the first vocational institution to provide specialised culinary education, was founded by the Woman's Educational Association of Boston (Brown, 2005); an interesting origin considering the profession's renowned male dominance. The school's mission was to teach low-income women the theoretical principles and scientific approaches to cooking, most of which can still be found in contemporary culinary arts programmes. In 1896, Fannie Farmer, the school principal, published the *Boston Cooking-School Cookbook*, which became the best-selling cookbook of the era. By the early years of the 20th century, the development and expansion of vocational education, along with the establishment of relevant institutions, helped to legitimise this form of education, earning it both industry and community support (Vanlandingham, 1995). Other notable institutions offering culinary programmes included Johnson & Wales University in Providence, Rhode Island (est. 1913), the Washburne Trade School in Chicago (est. 1937), and the Restaurant Institute of Connecticut, which was established in 1946 (now known as the Culinary Institute of America).

The formation of the American Culinary Federation (ACF) in 1929 was perhaps the most important development in solidifying the status of the culinary arts as a profession, thus validating the need for formal education. Nevertheless, the acceptance of culinary arts as an academic discipline had a long road ahead; it was only in 1986 that the ACF established accreditation procedures for culinary programmes. Encapsulating the above, Figure 4.3 exhibits a timeline of the evolution of culinary education.

Over the next three decades, and partially fuelled by the celebrity phenomenon, culinary programmes experienced an unprecedented growth at a global scale (Hertzman & Maas, 2012; Zopiatis et al., 2014). Hundreds of new programmes and dozens of newly established tertiary institutions now strive to educate the next generation of industry professionals.

Culinary programmes in non-traditional educational settings

Notably, culinary programmes are also offered in non-traditional educational settings, such as prisons, the military, and non-profit entities. Such programmes provide individuals with the opportunity to gain accreditation (e.g., NVQs Levels 1–3 in the UK) in food preparation and service. Especially with regards to prisons, such vocational programmes are ideal for reducing recidivism (reoffending), acquiring transferable skills, and strengthening post-release employment motivation and opportunities

Figure 4.3 Timeline of culinary education

(Bahn, 2011; Vineetha & Raghavan, 2018). An indicative example is the programme offered by The Clink,[1] a UK-based charity that works in partnership with the national prison service. The programme, which espouses the principles of social gastronomy and uses the power of food as a tool for social change, provides prisoners specialised training and mentoring, as well as post-release guidance and support.

According to official figures published by the UK Ministry of Justice (see The Clink Charity Yearbook, 2018), such programmes reduce recidivism by 50%; an astounding accomplishment compared to similar vocational programmes. Giousmpasoglou et al. (2019) explored trainee inmates' motivations, the most important emerging as: "to occupy my time usefully" (94.5%); "to challenge myself" (83.3%); "to improve my employment prospects on release" (80.6%); "to make my family proud of me" (77.7%); "to pursue an interest" (75.1%); and "to get a qualification" (72.3%). With regards to the primary benefits of such training, the same study revealed the following: "self-esteem/confidence" (91.6%); "ability/ desire to learn" (83.3%); "ability to help others" (83.3%); "health and wellbeing" (83.3%); "chances of getting a job" (80.6%); "ability to cope with prison" (75%); "communication skills" (72.3%); and "outlook on life and future" (72.2%).

The culinary curriculum

With roots in the vocational training paradigms of the previous two centuries (Mandabach et al., 2002), and especially John Dewey's (1938) vocationalism, contemporary culinary education, at least in theory, attempts to provide a balanced pedagogic experience that meets personal vocational aspirations, stakeholders' expectations, and the everchanging needs of the industry (e.g., changes in food consumption patterns, food technology, etc.). Dewey (1938) defines both the role and responsibilities of the "vocational" educator and provides a set of good practices aimed at enhancing the educational experience. His work has influenced the contributions of other notable scholars and theorists, such as Kurt Lewin and David Kold, and helped develop the theoretical foundation of contemporary vocational education.

As expected, Dewey's work on vocational education drew criticism as being outdated and unable to capture the narrative of this era mainly because it originated "from within a particular social and ideological context and was a response to early twentieth-century social, industrial, and economic conditions" (Franzosa, 1997, p. 172). Others highlight the identity problems surrounding vocational education, as well as the superficial approach taken by some institutions on how to deliver such an educational experience to students (DeFalco, 2016). DeFalco (p. 63) concludes by arguing that:

> Instead of vocational education being a peripheral concern of reformers, a superficial reference, it might yet become an education that will integrate social, political and moral issues along with reform in curriculum and methodology. The result? Individuals who are intelligent workers in charge of their own economic destiny.

Reflecting on the above, the debate is clearly ongoing amongst scholars (see Hu et al., 2006) as to the status of tertiary culinary education with regards to its pedagogic goals, objectives, structure, curriculum content, and quality indicators.

Undoubtedly, the long-standing utilisation of the master–apprentice model of vocational education has cultivated some deep-rooted beliefs (and mentalities) as to the nature and scope of the culinary educational experience. For centuries, the focus has been on practical and technical skills, which many have labelled as vocational (hands-on, applied skills) and not academic (theory-based). Consequently, the ambiguities around and divide between these two educational paradigms continue to impede the acceptance of culinary arts as a valid academic discipline (Hegarty & Antun, 2010). We can also safely assume the problem is exacerbated by the well-known negative connotations traditionally attached to vocational education, namely social image problems, "downgraded" curricula, and the propensity to attract students with below-average academic qualifications (Lynch, 2000).

In order to gain an in-depth understanding of the issues surrounding vocational culinary education, it is important to review the relevant professions from a historical and social context. Culinary professions have always been a "safe haven" for the traditionally disenfranchised who tended to serve the dominant social classes. A brief foray into the evolution of culinary arts education (e.g., master–apprentice relationships, guilds, programmes supporting the underprivileged, etc.) proves that these were jobs of necessity in support of basic human physiological needs, at least in the early stages, rather than a conscious and well-informed vocational choice. Encapsulating this notion, celebrity chef Anthony Bourdain (1956–2018) provided a colourful explanation, suggesting that "traditionally [chefs] were the losers of the family. It is a profession that has been welcoming to misfits throughout history". It is therefore logical and expected that such professions suffer from an image and reputation problem, especially with regards to their broad portrayal as unattractive, inhumane, anti-social, with below-average remuneration, and a multitude of work-life imbalances (Pratten & O'Leary, 2007); all vocational traits that discourage the academically gifted from pursuing careers in this field.

Liberal vs vocational: theory and practice

Responding to the above, scholars (see Lugosi et al., 2009) have highlighted the need to espouse a blended liberal and vocational approach in educating future culinary professionals. The need stems from the awareness that the narrative of this era requires culinary practitioners that possess well-rounded knowledge, skills, and abilities (KSAs) which far exceed the traditional 18th-century cookery requirements, which tended to focus on production and skill acquisition. Taking this notion further, Cairns et al. (2000, p. 34) elegantly note that:

> We need to overcome the false and sterile opposition of academic and vocational... Curricula should be designed with a view to eliminating the distinctions between academic and vocational; young people need aspects of both traditions. ... We need curriculum which gets beyond thinking in academic and vocational terms.

Calls for change and the adoption of a new – more liberal – framework for culinary arts education are clear, current, and ongoing. Such a change nevertheless necessitates a fundamental paradigm shift in culinary arts. Scholars supporting this notion suggest that culinary arts should be viewed as a social and not just a commercial act (Lashley & Morrison, 2000). Echoing the same notion, others theorise that changes needed to make culinary education more "liberal", or balanced, must aim towards the cultivation of a free human being, with suggested requirements ranging from critical (self-)reflection, communication, to innovation and creativity (Mitchell et al., 2013).

Despite the calls around the need to balance the two educational paradigms, actual practices suggest the opposite holds true in reality. Most programmes, in contrast to the literature that highlights the curriculum requirements for a successful culinary career, are overly focused towards nurturing the technical aspects of the profession (Muller et al., 2009). Even institutions who attempted to achieve some balance espouse a rather superficial approach; for example, the move to include a single three-hour course on innovation and entrepreneurship in a three-year culinary curriculum is at best ineffective. Hegarty (2004) highlights this disparity by suggesting that, in their current state, culinary curricula fail to meet the needs of the business world. This can be traced to problems in contextualising vocational knowledge, the relative scarcity of quality indicators, and the widespread gaps in the industry–education relationship. With regards to the latter, and despite the extensive experiential learning components of culinary programmes, differences between the "world of work" and education contribute to the skills gap phenomenon (see Chapter 5), which in turn poses unprecedented challenges for industry stakeholders.

In support of the aforementioned, and for purely indicative purposes, we explored the curriculum of 12 respected institutions in the US,[2] which combined offer 69 culinary programmes. Six institutions were specialised vocational schools, four were colleges, and two were universities. Thematically, the curriculum offerings were dissected into five broad categories: basic culinary/ baking/pastry (CBP); business related; liberal arts (communication, psychology, etc.); other electives; and internships. Overall, in specialised vocational and college institutions, the CBP courses exceed 60% of the curriculum, whereas the credit hours of liberal arts offerings are less than 10%. In contrast, the overall curriculum offered by universities – for all three specialisations – includes 40% basic CBP courses and 30% liberal arts and other electives. We note that in all cases the experiential component of students' pedagogic experience ranges from 10–20% of the overall credit hours. Finally, when comparing the degrees offered, we can identify a similar curriculum structure and course allocation in Culinary Arts, and Baking and Pastry, whereas Food Business/ Operations Management programmes exhibit a significantly different design with the inclusion of more business-related courses.

Programmes offered by specialised vocational schools and colleges (see Figure 4.4), regardless of their specialisation, exhibit significant differences

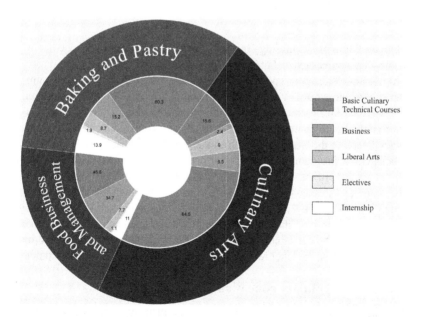

Figure 4.4 Culinary programmes in vocational schools and colleges

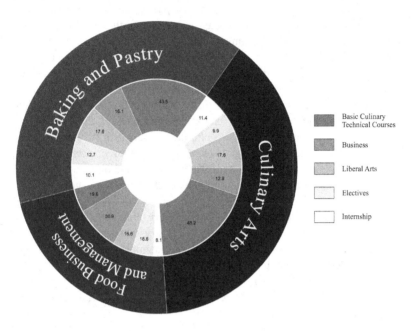

Figure 4.5 Culinary programmes in universities

compared to similar offerings by universities (see Figure 4.5). Specifically, basic CBP courses exceed 60% for Culinary Arts and the Baking and Pastry programmes offered in vocational schools and colleges, whereas this number drops below 50% in universities. In contrast, liberal arts courses offered by university programmes (all specialisations) exceed 17% of the curriculum credit hours compared to less than 9% in vocational schools and colleges. Notable differences are also evident with Food Business/Operations Management programmes offered by universities, in which basic CBP courses fall under 20% of the curriculum, whereas in vocational schools and colleges this number exceeds 45%. A similar picture is noted with elective courses, since universities, by exploiting the well-established synergies with other programmes, provide their students with a wider selection of choices that reach 19% of the curriculum credit hours, compared to only 1% offered by other institutions; the latter revealing the fixed structure of such programmes.

Quality and culinary education

Despite the vast conceptual background provided by the educational disciplines, only a handful of studies have explored the quality indicators of culinary education; a scarcity that enhances the overall ambiguity surrounding such programmes. In the educational context, Zopiatis et al. (2014, p. 89) define quality "as the characteristics of the learning experience able to meet or exceed the implied or stated needs and expectations of students, their families, the industry, and society". Indicators are the contextual factors that affect learning and define both the success of and satisfaction with the educational experience. These are, or should be, part of a holistic quality management system that enables the monitoring, control, evaluation, and improvement of both the curriculum, and organisational norms and policies, as well as internalisation via mobility and recognition of foreign qualifications.

Most culinary-specific research on quality indicators has been conducted by Jean L. Hertzman, a renowned US culinary educator. Working closely with the American Culinary Federation (ACF) and other colleagues, she conducted a number of studies with the aim of illuminating the quality indicators of relevant programmes, thus providing industry stakeholders valuable insight as to the key factors that define success. Hertzman and Stefanelli (2008) in particular investigated both educators and chefs, concluding that the five most important culinary indicators are: sanitation of kitchen laboratories; industry experience of faculty; subject experience of faculty; obligatory internships; and placement rates. In a later study (Hertzman & Ackerman, 2010), the list was amended to include 20 quality indicators related to categories such as faculty; organisation and administration; facilities; learning opportunities; student outcomes and related services; and resources. More recently, and by reflecting on the work of Hertzman and colleagues, Zopiatis et al. (2014) identified three important factors that define quality in culinary education, namely faculty and programme recognition, resources/facilities, and students and support services. The study found faculty and programme recognition to be the most influential factor in determining overall satisfaction with a culinary education. It includes, amongst others, indicators such as industry experience of faculty; faculty experience in subject/area taught; faculty participation in continuing education; and national accreditation.

Additional quality-related problems, such as the inherent difficulties in evaluating the vocational aspects of culinary educational experiences (Hertzman & Ackerman, 2010) and the risk of nurturing an academic bubble which may endanger the sustainability of the profession, thus causing a multitude of problems for the industry (Zopiatis, 2010), are also highlighted. With regards to the latter, it is important to note that the role of celebrities in nurturing unrealistic culinary vocational expectations has also been criticised, with Zopiatis and Melanthiou (2019) arguing that the danger of promoting a catastrophic new paradigm, a "Pedagogy of the Delusional...

where television, social media and the celebrity status of individuals nurture a distorted picture of both the values and norms of a particular profession" (p. 549), is higher than ever. Echoing the above, celebrity chef Bobby Flay highlights the risk of eroding the profession's very nature and core values by noting that his culinary students more often ask "How can I get my own show?" as opposed to "How can I learn to make great food?" (cited in Zopiatis & Melanthiou, 2019).

Culinary education programmes

Some of the best culinary programmes in the world tend to be offered by specialised vocational training schools. Reputable institutions include the Culinary Institute of America, the Auguste Escoffier School of Culinary Arts in the US, the Culinary Arts Academy in Switzerland, and Le Cordon Bleu in Paris, France, whereas the most renowned university-level culinary programmes can be found at Johnson & Wales University in Providence, Rhode Island. Taking advantage of globalisation, as well as the recent surge in the popularity and demand for relevant programmes, most of these institutions have pursued an aggressive internalisation strategy mostly via franchising agreements, and as a result already operate campuses in multiple locations and have plans to expand in Asia. These institutions offer a wide variety of programmes, ranging from one-year certifications all the way to four-year bachelor's degrees. The most popular certification and diploma degrees are Culinary Arts, and Pastry and Baking, whereas bachelor's degrees are in Food Business/Operations Management (see for example Johnson & Wales University programmes). For purely indicative purposes, Table 4.1 exhibits the most reputable culinary schools in the world.

As of 2019, 2,522 (n=2,522) culinary arts and chef training programmes were offered in the US.[3] Tuition costs vary across the board, nevertheless, and as suggested by Hertzman and Maas (2012), studying culinary arts does not tend to be an inexpensive proposition, especially in private institutions. The average tuition by an in-state public institution is just under $7,000 (median=$3,635), whereas the average fees by out-of-state private institutions amount to more than $10,000 (median=$19,504).[4] The average age of the individuals pursuing these programmes is 38 (most common ages are 30 and 32), with 51.1% being female; associate (two-year) degrees are the most popular (44%), followed by post-secondary certificates (one or two years; 27.9%), and certifications of less than one year (24.3%). Notably, only 2.5% of those pursuing culinary arts in the US graduated with a four-year bachelor's degree in 2019.

In Europe, culinary arts programmes are mostly offered by specialised institutions following the traditional Swiss-French vocational approach,

Table 4.1 Reputable culinary schools

Institution (location)	Ranking*						
	Chef's Pencil Culinary News[1]	The Best Culinary Schools[2]	College Rank[3]	The Kitchen Community[4]	Besttoppers[5]	GradLime[6]	Cooking School[7]
Auguste Escoffier School of Culinary Arts (Austin, Texas, US) www.escoffier.edu/	1	4	8	1	10	6	
Culinary Arts Academy (Switzerland) https://www.culinaryartsswitzerland.com/en/	2			4			
The Culinary Institute of America (Multiple Locations) www.ciachef.edu/	3	1 (NY)	2 (CA) & 5 (NY)	2	1 (NY) 2 (CA)	3	9
Le Cordon Bleu (35 locations across 5 continents) www.cordonbleu.edu/home/en	4 (Paris, FR)		7	3 (Paris, FR)	3		5
Institute of Culinary Education (New York, US) www.ice.edu/	5	2	1	5	4	1	
Apicius (Florence, Italy) https://apicius.it/	6			8			
Westminster Kingsway College (London, UK) https://www.westking.ac.uk/	7			6			
Kendall College School of Culinary Arts (Chicago, USA) https://kendallcollege.nl.edu/	8	8	4		7	4	3
BHMS (Lucerne, Switzerland) www.bhms.ch/	9	9	6	9	9	5	6
New England Culinary Institute (Montpelier, Vermont, US) www.neci.edu/	10			9		9	
Henry Ford College (Dearborn, Michigan, US) www.hfcc.edu/			9				

(Continued)

Table 4.1 (Continued)

Institution (location)	Ranking*						
	Chef's Pencil Culinary News[1]	The Best Culinary Schools[2]	College Rank[3]	The Kitchen Community[4]	Besttoppers[5]	GradLime[6]	Cooking School[7]
Paul Bocuse Institute (Lyon, France) https://en.institutpaulbocuse.com/				7			
Johnson and Wales University (Providence, RI; North Miami; Denver; and Charlotte) https://www.jwu.edu/		6 (RI)			8 (RI)	7 (RI)	2
Culinary Institute of Barcelona (Barcelona, Spain) https://cib.education/en	12						
Hattori Nutrition College (Tokyo, Japan) http://global.hattori.ac.jp/	13						

Sources: *all data retrieved in June–July 2021.

[1] www.chefspencil.com/13-best-culinary-schools-in-the-world/
[2] https://thebestschools.org/rankings/certificates/best-culinary-schools/
[3] www.collegerank.net/best-culinary-programs/
[4] https://thekitchencommunity.org/worlds-best-culinary-schools/
[5] https://besttoppers.com/top-10-culinary-schools/
[6] https://gradlime.com/culinary-arts-schools/
[7] www.cookingschool.org/top-schools/

which entails up to 50% practical experience in either the industry or purpose-built, in-house restaurants and labs.[5] Famous tertiary vocational institutions include the Paul Bocuse Institute in Lyon, France; Le Cordon Bleu in Paris, France (as well as in another 35 locations worldwide); the Culinary Arts Academy in Le Bouveret, Switzerland; and Apicius in Florence, Italy. In the UK, well-known institutions offering culinary programmes include both colleges and universities, for example the Westminster Kingsway College in London, the University of Derby in Buxton, and the College of Food and Hospitality Management at University College Birmingham. It is important to note that, especially in the UK, institutions tend to follow a more business-oriented approach, with the inclusion of courses relevant to food operations management.

The questionable value of culinary education

The necessity and value of culinary arts education at all levels (especially regarding the four-year bachelor's degree) and specialisations is another contested topic. According to Hertzman and Ackerman (2010), less than half of food and beverage workers have some form of formal tertiary education, with the preferred programmes being two-year associate degrees. We note that most food and beverage jobs are classified as entry-level positions, thus no formal education and training is required, potentially save for upper-scale luxury establishments. The premise is that, via in-house, on-the-job training and experience, the employee will master the KSAs needed to meet the established quality standards of the operation, and if possible, to be promoted internally to a junior supervisory position. This approach reflects the ongoing debate as to whether experience is more important than formal education in hospitality (including culinary) professions.

Up until the 1970s, many industry stakeholders argued that actual workplace experience is far more important than formal hospitality education. It was believed that the only way someone could become a successful hospitality professional was by experiencing all levels and job classifications of the establishment. Traditionally, a hospitality employee would commence their career in either the Food and Beverage or the Rooms Division and then, after years of hard work, personal sacrifices, and perseverance, earn a promotion to a junior managerial position (Giousmpasoglou, 2012). The focus was mainly on technical skills, since attention to detail was considered, especially in the Swiss-French educational system, the key element to service delivery and profitability. Consequently, managerial skills such as human resources; interpersonal communication; problem-solving; strategic planning and decision making; financial control; teamwork; delegation; and leadership took a back seat and were – unrealistically – expected to be passed on via on-the-job interaction with senior hospitality managers, who themselves lacked formal education. Consequently, the managerial deficiencies of senior managers were passed on to junior managers, thus shaping an inadequate, "cloned" management style fuelled by autocratic behaviour, subjectivity, and a lack of adequate financial control, delegation skills, and strategic perspective.

In contrast, most culinary positions are considered to be skilled, especially in upscale establishments, thus formal tertiary education is highly recommended for career success and progression. Nevertheless, and as reported by Hertzman and Maas (2012), many challenge the cost–value proposition of culinary education, especially the one offered in private, for-profit institutions. Their findings revealed that factors such as the rising cost of such programmes, cumbersome student loans, and insufficient post-graduation returns (e.g., starting position or salary) severely challenge the necessity and value of the learning experience on offer. Nevertheless, some reject this quantitative cost–benefit approach by suggesting that, while the career starting point might be the same for all, career progression and ultimate level of professional success might be completely different depending on the individual.

Echoing the above sentiment, Alison Arnett (2018) highlights the challenges facing culinary arts education, and the institutions offering such specialised programmes.

Conclusion

Historians often argue that the 21st century is an era of major social change due to the transition from an industrial to a knowledge-based society. The critical factor in this emerging society is our ability to develop new kinds of knowledge in a highly demanding and constantly changing global environment. Education must respond with pedagogical strategies that ensure students are adequately equipped to meet the new challenges. Stakeholders expect well-rounded individuals that possess the necessary, current, and diverse KSAs that will enable them to effectively contribute to operational success, challenge deep-rooted paradigms, and guide this sector further into the 21st century. Culinary education must strive to develop a pedagogically sound and holistic educational experience, one that reflects the modern realities of the relevant professions and provides talented individuals the foundation for a successful culinary career.

Notes

1 See https://theclinkcharity.org/.
2 See https://thebestschools.org/rankings/best-culinary-schools/.
3 See https://datausa.io/profile/cip/culinary-arts-chef-training.
4 See https://datausa.io/profile/cip/culinary-arts-chef-training.
5 See https://www.chefspencil.com/best-20-culinary-schools-in-europe/.

5 Skills and competencies for chefs

Introduction

The success or failure of any profession depends on the knowledge, skills, and abilities (KSAs) – and talents – of its employees, especially in a human-centred, labour-intensive industry such as tourism. Employees are without a doubt a determining factor in organisational success, both at a micro and macro level, thus demand for the ideal employee has been, and remains, a pressing issue. Reflecting the industry's competitive nature, hospitality operators engage in fierce wars to attract the most talented individuals to their ranks. Nevertheless, and despite the plethora of relevant scholarly investigations, as well as optimistic proclamations, reality suggests that the industry still makes for a mediocre workplace. As a result, the collective

DOI: 10.4324/9781003160250-5

ability to attract the most talented individuals is minimal (Zopiatis et al., 2018).

Reprising his 2007 work, Tom Baum, a renowned hospitality Human Resources Management (HRM) academic, reflected on the status of human resource practices in tourism by illuminating emerging issues that may influence the industry's labour force, and consequently the quest for the ideal employee. As noted, hospitality is still perceived as a low-skill sector, which according to the dual labour market theory, falls under the secondary sector: low-status jobs with below-average working conditions and remuneration, questionable job security, and limited opportunities for promotion. Furthermore, Baum (2015) notes that the introduction of new business models (e.g., outsourcing) may change the landscape of the conventional "front" and "back" of the house hospitality jobs, whereas deskilling in major functional areas – mostly due to technological advancements – will reduce the demand for employees with traditional technical skills, especially in the post-COVID-19 era. Adding to this discourse, the industry's renowned human resources practices further restrict the capacity to attract employees who are a good fit. High employee turnover, leadership deficits, seasonality, overdependence on non-traditional labour markets, gender issues (e.g., glass ceiling), burnout, employee shortages, work–life (im)balance, the skills gap, and nepotism are just some of the most common challenges cited in the international literature (Baum, 2007, 2015; Pratten, 2003a & b; Pratten & O'Leary, 2007; Zopiatis et al., 2018).

Fuelled by the narrative of this era, food and beverage, and especially culinary operations, are perhaps the only sector of the contemporary hospitality industry not facing problems with attracting individuals to its ranks, at least in numbers. Since the early 2000s, for example, global enrolment in culinary tertiary programmes has been on the rise, with new institutions opening their doors to a multi-generational audience who each envision either a prosperous career (including a mid-life career change for non-traditional students) or a lucrative rise in status to become a celebrity chef. As expected, this unprecedented and, for some, unsustainable growth drew severe criticism, with Zopiatis (2010, p. 461) noting that:

This remarkable growth … could potentially create a generation of unemployed culinary school graduates. Other stakeholders doubt whether the industry is able to absorb such vast numbers of graduates in such a short period of time and whether academia is able to adequately prepare them to enter and successfully contribute towards operational success.

Reflecting the above, it is vital for culinary stakeholders to embrace a quality-over-quantity mentality, in which the most talented individuals are identified, attracted by the industry's core values, recruited, and then developed, via education and training, to actively contribute to the service delivery process. The first step towards such an endeavour is to target the ideal employee, which includes defining the objective and measurable KSAs according to both the industry's and the market's everchanging demands. The volatile nature of this quest is noted, since KSAs deemed necessary two decades ago might no longer match up to the industry's needs. This could be due to changes, amongst others, in culinary specificities, consumer behaviour and habits, technology, and unanticipated external events.

Towards a definition of competencies

Exploring the KSAs required of the ideal employee is perhaps one of the most popular research themes in hospitality and tourism literature, including culinary literature; the latter is a field that, despite carrying a vast conceptual potential and interest, has a vocational nature that still discourages many scholars from pursuing relevant studies. Job competencies have received extensive coverage in generic business literature, with Boyatzis (1982, pp. 20–21) defining them as "an underlying characteristic of a person which results in effective and/or superior performance in a job". Culinary scholars have added to this discourse, with Zopiatis (2010, p. 460) defining competencies as "the personal qualities and talents needed to do a pre-described job effectively and efficiently according to established quantifiable organizational standards able to meet specific goals", while Suhairom et al. (2019, p. 206) describe them as "measurable patterns of knowledge, skills, abilities, behaviours and other characteristics that differentiate high from average performance".

Competency frameworks

Over recent decades, scholars have developed numerous theoretical frameworks that dissect competencies according to their distinct characteristics. As exhibited in Table 5.1, and reflecting the narrative of each era, a variety of generic competency frameworks have been introduced in the world of business. Conceptual similarities are noted, since almost all of these studies were influenced, to a certain degree, by prior literature. Moreover, we note the distinctive differences between business-related competency frameworks and others (e.g., frameworks for educators or medical doctors), each reflecting the idiosyncrasies of their specific industry.

In retrospect, perhaps the most influential framework was that introduced by Sandwith (1993, pp. 46–50) who categorised competencies into five themes, namely: conceptual-creative (cognitive skills associated with comprehending important elements of the job and creative thought);

Table 5.1 Generic (business) competency frameworks

Author(s)	Competency categories	Field
McClelland (1973)	Social, interpersonal, leadership	Generic Business
Katz (1974)	Technical, human, conceptual	Generic Business
Umbreit (1992)	Leadership, human resource management, marketing, financial analysis, total quality management, communication skills	Generic Business
Alderson (1993)	Interpersonal relationships, openness, trust, approachability, discipline, and cohesion	Generic Business
Sandwith (1993)	Conceptual-Creative, leadership, interpersonal, administrative, technical	Generic Business
Nordhaug (1998)	Task-specific, firm-specific, and industry-specific	Generic Business
Van den Berg (1998)	Knowledge, behavioural style, cognitive capacity, personality	Generic Business
Rainsbury et al. (2002)	Technical, analytical, constructive, and appreciative skills	Generic Business
Koenigsfeld et al. (2012)	Conceptual, leadership, administrative, interpersonal, technical (inspired by the work of Sandwith, 1993)	Generic Business/ Club
Al Mamun et al. (2019)	Entrepreneurial skills, market orientations, sales orientations, networking, entrepreneurial competency, micro-enterprise performance	Generic Business

leadership (the ability to turn ideas into productive action); interpersonal (skills for effective interaction with others); administrative (human resource and financial aspects of organisational life); and technical (knowledge and skills associated with the actual work). This work has inspired a number of studies and has become a point of reference for various industries, including hospitality and tourism. Almost all subsequent frameworks include the categories of technical and interpersonal competencies, with some variations on the leadership and administrative themes, with either the inclusion of a broader management category (Testa & Sipe, 2012) or more specific terms such as entrepreneurial skills (see Al Mamun et al., 2019).

In hospitality and tourism, and mostly reflecting the operational and vocational traits of the relevant professions, scholars have developed several frameworks (see Table 5.2). Almost all studies have been produced post-2000 and either pursue a generic one-size-fits-all approach or focus

Table 5.2 Hospitality competency frameworks

Author(s)	Competency Categories	Field
Birdir and Pearson (2000)	Communication, planning, organising, ability to make decisions	Culinary
Kay and Russette (2000)	Leadership, interpersonal, conceptual – creative, administrative, and technical skills	Hotels
Hu (2010)	Culture, aesthetic, technology, product, service, management, creativity	Culinary
Zopiatis (2010)	Technical (culinary-specific), conceptual (creative-adaptive), interpersonal, administrative (budget and strategic planning, and professional administrative strengths), and leadership-management (leadership strengths, management skills)	Culinary
Giousmpasoglou (2012)	Intellectual, personal, communication, interpersonal, leadership, result performance	Hotels
Testa and Sipe (2012)	Business oriented: planning, continuous improvement, strategic decision making, systems thinking, technical service, results oriented People oriented: interpersonal communication, expressive service, team orientation, coaching and training, inspiration, cultural alignment, networked Self-oriented: accountability, professionalism, self-development, time management, spirit of optimism, change management	Hospitality & Tourism
Gersh (2016)	Administrative, leadership, conceptual, interpersonal, technical	Culinary
Allen and Mac Con Iomaire (2017)	Professionalism, individual characteristics, management, leadership	Culinary
Wan et al. (2017)	Behavioural, operational, management skills	Culinary
Lou et al. (2019)	Cognitive, functional, meta-competency, social	Hotels
Dolasinski and Reynolds (2019)	Soft skill, leadership, interpersonal, organisational, relational, self-management	Hotel
Suhairom et al. (2019)	Technical, non-technical, personal quality, physical state, motive, self-concept	Culinary
Marinakou and Giousmpasoglou (2020)	Management/leadership, technical, strategic, operational	Culinary
Marneros et al. (2020)	Leadership, financial analysis, human resource management, human relations – communication, operational knowledge	Hotel

on specific sectors of the industry. Reflecting on generic business frameworks, these studies attempt to preserve the nature of the industry while also maintaining the necessary balance between skills that are soft (relevant to personality traits) and those that can be described as hard (technical, job-specific, learnable). Soft skills include interpersonal, human, people, or behavioural traits (some terms are used interchangeably) mostly associated with those with a liberal arts education. According to Weber et al. (2013), soft skills can be dissected into (a) leadership/people/relationship skills, (b) communication, (c) management/organisation, and (d) cognitive skills and competencies. In contrast, hard skills in the hospitality contexts include foreign language skills, technology proficiency, and a variety of technical skills relevant to day-to-day operations (e.g., food and beverage services, culinary production, sanitation and safety tasks, housekeeping, engineering, and maintenance). Finally, both skill types are transferable, in that they can be applied in a variety of horizontal and vertical career paths, as well as other professions.

Hard skills are considered more specific, thus can easily be defined and taught, whereas soft skills are closely related to the individual's personality and consequent behaviour, both elements that cannot be easily modified. Espousing this notion, the industry's traditional recruitment motto has been to identify individuals with the "right" personality, per job classification, and then pay attention to other notable KSAs and prior experience. Nevertheless, this motto has in practice proven to be insufficient, since candidates tend to be over-prepared in addressing such issues during the interviewing process; in short, they value their true personality. As a result, even with the utilisation of elaborate interviewing techniques and sophisticated psychometric tools, the likelihood of selecting the "wrong" candidate, the precursor of (in)voluntary turnover, following a 15–20 minute interview, remains relatively high. In this equation, we must also consider other recruitment elements, such as the size of the labour pool, the direct cost of turnover (and employee replacement), and the indirect cost of variation in service quality; the latter having a direct effect on customer experience.

A closer look at these competency frameworks (see Table 5.2) reveals that, despite methodological differences, there are also noteworthy similarities. Reflecting on the vocational nature of the industry, almost all studies include technical competencies, thus verifying the importance of operational knowledge to perform day-to-day tasks. Soft skills are also noted, with competencies relevant to communication, interpersonal skills, behavioural elements, and human skills, amongst others. With regards to management – more evident in hotel-specific studies – categories include management/leadership competencies and administrative competencies (e.g., financial planning, cost control, etc.). Notable is the fact that only one culinary-specific study (Hu, 2010) categorised creativity as a primary competency, even though others (see Horng & Hu, 2008) consider creative skills as the cornerstone of contemporary culinary arts. We note that, while creativity is the basis for innovation and entrepreneurship, vital for today's food and beverage Small & Medium Enterprises (SMEs), in the culinary context, this is mostly understood as the artistic element in food production.

Culinary skills and competencies: a review

To review existing frameworks, we turn to a handful of studies, most notably the work of Sandwith (1993), that highlight the skills and competencies required to succeed in culinary operations. As exhibited in Table 5.3 (see also Vogel et al., 2021), frameworks vary mostly due to the methodological heterogeneities of each study, and especially the variations and overlapping definitions of competency terms utilised; elements that restrict any valid comparison and conclusions. Most studies explore the views of culinary professionals in a variety of positions, some involve educators, while only one (Marinakou & Giousmpasoglou, 2020) investigates the perceptions of culinary students. With regards to ranking, some studies elevate technical skills as the most important (Zopiatis, 2010), whereas others prioritise professionalism, leadership, and management/administration (Allen & Mac Con Iomaire, 2017), or interpersonal skills (Gersh, 2016). Finally, differences between stakeholders – mostly culinary professionals and educators – are noted (see Marinakou & Giousmpasoglou, 2020), nevertheless we caution that the utilised small sample sizes prohibit us from reaching any definite and generalisable conclusions.

In addition to the issue of sample size, it is important to acknowledge other limitations of these culinary studies and their proposed competency frameworks. These studies are in their majority cross-sectional, capturing the views of a specific population at a given point in time. The absence of longitudinal research designs (re-examining the same subjects over an extended period) severely restricts the ability to compare different eras and identify trends and changes in culinary-specific competencies, especially as these relate to developments in culinary arts, technology, and unanticipated external events. Next, most of these studies are investigating the views and opinions of culinary professionals and educators with regards to current – and not future – industry needs. By their publication date, usually 12–18 months after the field study, such endeavours may already be outdated. Moreover, this static approach – "what is important today?" – fails to provide a forward-looking, holistic perspective of what the industry will need in five or ten years. If we take into consideration the slow pace of academia's reflective qualities in responding to current industry needs, then

Table 5.3 Culinary competency frameworks

Author (s)	Zopiatis (2010)	Wan et al. (2017)	Marinakou and Giousmpasoglou (2020)
Country	Cyprus	Taiwan	UK
Method	Quantitative	Qualitative	Quantitative
Instrument used – conceptual influence	Descriptive and Inferential Statistics/Conceptual influence from Sandwith (1993), five-point Likert scale (5=extremely important,4= very important 3=important, 2=slightly important and 1=not important)	Focus group interviews, in-depth interviews, Delphi Method/Conceptual influence from Soderquiest et al. (2010)	Descriptive Statistics, Exploratory Factor Analysis/Conceptual influence from Zopiatis (2010), five-point Likert scale (1 for not important to 5 for extremely important)
Sample	N=92 (Chefs)	N=15 (Executive Chefs and Sous Chefs)	N=407 (1: Chefs / 2: Instructors / 3: Students)
Key Competencies	Technical (culinary-specific), Conceptual (creative-adaptive), Interpersonal competencies, Administrative competencies, Leadership-management competencies	Two dimensions: (1) Behaviour & Skill (2) Managerial & operational	Management/leadership, Technical, Strategic, Operational
	Mean	**Managerial Behaviour:** **Mean**	**Mean (1*,2*,3*)**
	Competencies Technical (culinary-specific) 4.55	Handling crisis skill 9.60	**Management/leadership:** 4.20(1) 4.40(2) 3.92(3)
	Knowledge of food service operations 4.55	Caring co-worker need 8.47	Human skills
	Knowledge of culinary flavours 4.73	Role model-type behaviour 8.87	Managerial skills
	Knowledge of recipe and menu development 4.62	Facilitating cooperation as a group 9.27	Ability to motivate
	Artistic culinary creativity 4.28	Having international viewpoint 9.20	Decision-making
		Encourage, motivate employee and values the contributions of all team members 9.07	Time management
			Professionalism
		Appreciating different culture 8.40	Handle staff complaints
			Adaptation to difficulty

(Continued)

Table 5.3 (Continued)

Author (s)	Zopiatis (2010)		Wan et al. (2017)		Marinakou and Giousmpasoglou (2020)	
	Conceptual (creative-adaptive)	**4.32**	**Operational Behaviour:**		Organisation skills	**4.13(1) 4.31(2) 3.73(3)**
	Ability to innovate	4.18	Keeps abreast of industry trends & metric	8.67	Communication	
	Ability to change	4.16	Regulating stress	9.30	Emotional control/ stability Staff appraisal	
	Adaptation to difficult circumstances	4.61	Innovation & view change as a way of life	8.87	**Technical**	
	Interpersonal competencies	**4.42**	Hold oneself accountable for results	9.40	Food preparation	
	Communication skills	4.53	Reputation oriented	9.67	Food safety	
	Verbal and writing skills	4.47	Displaying a positive persona and having energetic character	9.20	Recipe and menu development	
	Knowledge of diverse cultures	4.33	Managing emotions	9.20	Knowledge of flavour	
	Administrative competencies		**Managerial Skills:**	**4.42**	Artistic creativity	
	Budget and strategic planning	4.42	Staff training, dispatch and Work instruction	9.27	Sustainability/ waste management	
	Appreciation of cost management	4.69	Strategic management	8.67	Knowledge of food	
	Implementing labor cost controls	4.43	Organised and system oriented	9.07	Change	
	Budgeting	4.34	Revenue and performance management	9.29	**Strategic**	**3.82(1) 4.04(2) 3.49(3)**
	Knowledge of strategic planning	4.23	Implementation	9.40	Strategic planning	
	Professional administrative strengths	**4.43**			Labour cost control	
					Cost management	
					Budgeting	
					Innovate	

					3.83(1) 3.95(2) 3.76(3)
Time management	4.43	Communication skills	9.20	**Operational**	
Organisation skills	4.63	Having coordination skills	9.07	Verbal communication and writing	
Computer skills	4.25	**Operational Skills:**		Computer skills	
Leadership-management competencies		Knowledge of food safety and hygiene	9.07	Knowledge of cultures	
Leadership strengths	**4.45**	Cooking and meal research skills	9.07	Ethics / responsibility	
Decision making skills	4.69	Material and cost control	9.40	Emotional intelligence	
Ethical contact	4.35	Knowledge and control of raw material	9.13		
Emotional control and stability	4.18				
Emotional intelligence	4.28				
Professionalism	4.80				
Managerial skills	**4.48**				
Managerial skills (delegating and organising)	4.73				
Human skills	4.61				
Ability to motivate others	4.48				
Effectively handle staff complains	4.41				
Conduct staff appraisals	4.33				

Note: For a more thorough analysis of competency models in culinary arts please review Vogel et al. (2021)

it is easy to realise why this industry is facing a skills gap. Finally, the heterogeneity in methodological research designs and theoretical backgrounds of these studies severely diminishes our capabilities for defining the success competencies of culinary professions.

The skills gap phenomenon

A typical phenomenon in labour-intensive service professions like culinary arts is the skills gap. Defined as the mismatch (excess or deficit) between the required or expected skillset necessary for a particular job and what the individual employee actually possesses (CEDEFOP, 2012), this phenomenon challenges the industry's infamous "pair of hands" practices since employers are seeking qualified individuals that can effectively contribute to the service delivery operational processes as soon as they come on board (Box 5.1). Fuelled by technological advancements, the ongoing incongruence between formal education and the actual "world of work", the slow pace of academia's reflective qualities in adjusting to current and future needs, the industry's vulnerability to external micro and macro factors (economic crises, pandemics, incidents of political instability, etc.), as well as everchanging consumer behaviour, the skills gap poses unprecedented challenges for industry stakeholders. Despite the gap's operational importance, especially with regards to tertiary education and the industry's strategic training initiatives, the lack of research in this field is surprising.

BOX 5.1 SHORTAGE OF SKILLS IN THE CULINARY SECTOR

In April 2016 the Bureau of Labor Statistics reported that eight million Americans are unemployed, while at the same time 5.5 million jobs remain unfilled in America. This crisis exists because employers demand "job ready" employees and prospective employees are simply not able to bridge the skills gap without appropriate education and training.

Although restaurant-goers may not be aware of it, the restaurant industry in America is facing an ongoing problem: from New York to San Francisco, there is a shortage of skilled employees.

The need for skilled chefs and line cooks in America is growing rapidly. From 2004 to 2014, more new full-service restaurants opened than in any other part of the industry. In order to staff those restaurant kitchens, the Bureau of Labor Statistics projects that by 2025, nearly 200,000 more line cooks and chefs will be needed, according to *The*

New York Times. According to the National Restaurant Association, there will be 1.7 million new restaurant jobs created by 2026.

The most skilled culinary positions will grow faster than the rest of the American workforce. The Bureau of Labor Statistics projects that between 2014 and 2024 we will see a 9% growth in chefs and head cooks. Not only are kitchen positions in high demand, they also require middle skills – skills which employers have found to be lacking in the modern workforce. As the leading provider of culinary talent, private sector institutions will play an essential role in filling this gap. Unfortunately, the current gainful employment regulation is threatening this sector because most chefs begin their careers in the training stages of a career and thus early salaries do not reflect the median income of experienced professional chefs.

"Private sector colleges and universities confer more than half of all culinary degrees. At Stratford University, we work closely with employers to ensure graduates have the skills necessary to meet the culinary industry's growing demand. Through strong collaboration, we help graduates find better placements and help restaurants staff their kitchens with qualified professionals," said Richard R. Shurtz II, President, Stratford University. "More importantly, we prepare our graduates for promotion by embedding communication, problem solving, management, and team building skills into the curriculum."

Other specialised chefs, such as pastry chefs, will see a 7% growth over the same ten-year period.

Source: CESU (2016). Shortage of Skills:
The Culinary Sector. Available at: www.career.org/
n`ews/shortage-of-skills-the-culinary-sector

Hertzman and Stefanelli (2005) were amongst the first to acknowledge the existence of this phenomenon in the culinary profession, highlighting the rising danger of ill-prepared individuals unable to meet the industry's ever-changing needs, and thus exacerbating renowned recruitment problems, and consequently, (in)voluntary turnover. Despite suggestions and actions, mostly from academia, on how to mitigate the effects of the skills gap, industry stakeholders continue to highlight ongoing deficiencies in basic culinary technical skills (Sharma & Sharma, 2019). They argue that the academic shift towards more soft skills (liberal education) has developed at the expense of basic technical skills. Other scholars take a diametrically opposing view (see Muller et al., 2009), positing that culinary education is in fact overly focused on technical skills that reflect 18th-century cooking fundamentals, and is thus failing to produce well-rounded professionals able to meet the current and future needs of the industry (Hegarty, 2004).

These arguments may suggest a generalised and myopic view, in which industry stakeholders are only considering the early stages of the individual's progression, and thus neglecting vital KSAs necessary for a successful long-term career. Undoubtedly, hard technical competencies are often more essential during the early stages of a culinary career, pushing human and conceptual skills, at least initially, to the background. As progress is made towards the top of the profession, to become a chef – in essence a managerial position – or a culinary entrepreneur, soft skills become vital. Nevertheless, it is still unclear whether conventional culinary career progression paths enable the competency development of those skills necessary to reach these higher echelons. We also note that this ambiguity may be partially attributed to (a) the problematic comparison between culinary and other hospitality and tourism professions, (b) the vocational nature of culinary education, and (c) the unrealistic expectations of industry professionals as to the nature, scope, and depth of relevant tertiary education.

The competency framework for culinary professions

Reflecting on the existing theoretical background, we propose a balanced competency framework for culinary professions. This suggestion attempts to highlight the "success" KSAs, both current and future, that are required of the ideal culinary professional. Two premises must first be established. First, we acknowledge that a one-size-fits-all approach is unlikely to capture the idiosyncrasies of culinary job classifications across the board. It is critical to consider the specificities of each operation, e.g., the ownership type, organisational structure category, rating type (e.g., Michelin-star establishments), location, market, customers, menu, type of service, job classification, labour market, available career paths (vertical and horizontal), and the cultural and socio-economic setting of the organisation. And second, we consider not just the current professional requirements – the typical "what is necessary/essential today?" scenario depicted in the academic literature – but future ones as well.

The proposed framework (see Figure 5.1) includes five levels of KSAs and personal competencies that must be nurtured by a culinary professional envisioning to reach the top of the profession. We note that mastering one level is not a prerequisite for advancing to the next one, nevertheless, and as expected, KSAs are highly transferable from one level to the next. Level 1 consists of specific human and behavioural qualities essential for someone wishing to become a culinary professional. We particularly note ethics and integrity, interpersonal skills, aptitude, personality, willingness to learn, emotional

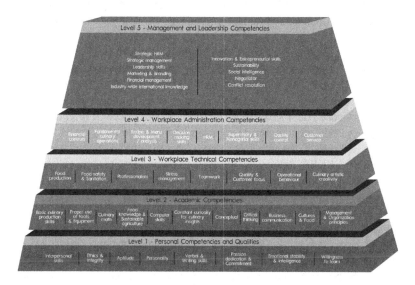

Figure 5.1 The balanced competency framework for culinary professions

stability and intelligence, and a genuine commitment and passion to pursue a career in this field. Level 2 includes qualities mostly nurtured in the academic environment, namely, basic culinary production skills, food knowledge (e.g., flavours and ingredients), cultures and food, fundamental understanding of sustainable agriculture (e.g., agribusiness and food production, national and international food standards, etc.), business communication skills, culinary maths, critical thinking, management/administration principles, organisational skills, computer skills, conceptual skills (creativity and adaptation), and constant curiosity for culinary insights (e.g., industry developments, trends, etc.). It is important to reiterate that not all culinary professionals pursue formal tertiary education, thus Level 2 KSAs can be – at least partially – nurtured in the workplace in the early stages of an employee's career.

Level 3 of the proposed framework includes workplace technical knowledge, mostly associated with entry-level culinary careers. Operational culinary skills (e.g., food preparation, food safety, and sanitation), teamwork, multitasking, quality and customer focus, professionalism, operational behaviour (time management, patience, resilience, stamina, interest to learn and absorb new knowledge, kitchen culture, etc.), and adaptation to change are just some of the desired KSAs of this level. The idea is to facilitate the smooth transition and assimilation of the new employee in the workplace and enable career progression.

Level 4 includes workplace administration KSAs mostly associated with operational-level supervisors. Recommended KSAs include knowledge of micro-operational financial controls (e.g., budgeting, food and beverage (F&B) and labour cost control, operational standards, etc.), fundamental culinary operations (e.g., purchasing, delivery/ inspection, storage, production, service, HACCP monitoring, etc.), recipe and menu development/ analysis, quality control, decision-making skills, organisational skills, and supervisory HRM skills (e.g., recruitment and selection of entry-level employees, training, monitoring, evaluating, disciplining).

Finally, Level 5, the upper echelon of this pyramid, entails managerial and leadership KSAs relevant to the macro-operational and strategic aspects of culinary operations. The skills that are highly recommended at this level are strategic planning, leadership skills, industry-wide knowledge, financial management, HRM (including recruitment of supervisors, delegation, managing diversity in a multicultural and multigenerational culinary workplace, coaching, mentoring, etc.), marketing and branding, sustainability, innovation, and entrepreneurial skills, and change management.

In a recent article (see Box 5.2), Sarah Taylor, a hospitality expert, highlighted the ten most essential skills needed to become a chef in the 21st century.

**BOX 5.2 TOP TEN SKILLS NEEDED
TO BECOME A CHEF**

No doubt, you need to be able to cook, but being a chef is more than putting food on a plate. You also need to develop and master some key skills. We've worked with chefs to develop a list of top ten skills that will help prepare you for a successful career as a chef.

1. **Willingness to learn:** Becoming a chef can be a hands-on learning experience, and like they say, practice does make perfect. You must master flavours and techniques of different dishes which can take time and a lot of energy. In order to become a great chef, you will need to be open to constant learning.
2. **Genuine passion:** The life of a chef is demanding as the busiest working days are often those when other people are out celebrating – Christmas, Valentine's Day, or Mothering Sunday, to name a few. Therefore you must have a real desire to be the person who makes other people's dining experiences special. Protecting and encouraging your passion for all things culinary will keep your artistic flair alive, and help you enjoy your work.

3. **Organisation:** We know that kitchens can be a very busy environment to work in, and so it is essential that you have the ability to always work clean and tidy. Take the time to tidy up as you go so that you don't get overwhelmed in your section, wipe your surfaces down and put everything back where it belongs. Stay organised to stay in control. As you progress in your career, having excellent organisational skills will ensure you manage staff effectively and help you to control every aspect of the kitchen, from the flow of work to the plating of dishes.

4. **Ability to skilfully multitask:** There can be many elements of food on one plate to make up a complete dish. Now think, that plate belongs on a table with three other mains, plus sides. If that table had starters as well, that's possibly four other previous dishes that need factoring in to how and when this one dish comes together. Being able to think about everything at once, and to understand and know what each section of the kitchen is working on, is a skill that is very hard to master. A head chef will be able to do this very well, they will also understand and know what the customers are experiencing, and what the front of the house team is doing at any point during service.

5. **Creativity:** Becoming a chef involves more than just following a recipe. A chef will be creative in terms of putting a menu together, how the dish looks on the plate, and how it tastes to the customers. They will also be creative in planning how the kitchen works. Some chefs will even take charge of décor, tableware, and seating arrangements in the restaurant. The creative reputation of a chef is often what brings customers through the door, so don't be afraid to experiment with your creativity!

6. **Time management:** Our sixth skill comes from Victor, who has over 15 years experience as a classically trained chef before setting up his own business in commercial kitchen design. Victor highlights the importance of time management; he says this skill has been additionally beneficial to him outside the kitchen.

7. **Teamwork:** The professional kitchen can be a melting pot of people, with many people from different backgrounds coming together through a shared love of cooking. Being able to both work and get on well with your team is an essential skill for a smooth cheffing career. Being a chef in a kitchen is like being a cog in a machine; every person has a role to play for the success

of the service. You and the rest of your team have to work together well in order to deliver this.

8. **Leadership skills:** As well as being a team player, experienced chefs should know how to lead the team, and get the best out of them. The head chef has the responsibility for the kitchen, and so they have to be able to give direction and have it followed immediately. At the same time, they need to maintain an upbeat atmosphere in the kitchen. They may also need to mentor and coach junior staff members during service, whilst ensuring everything runs smoothly.

9. **Resilience:** Chefs will frequently receive feedback from other chefs, colleagues, and customers on the food they produce, and not all of the feedback will be positive. You need to be able to handle criticism, look at it honestly, and decide whether or not it is valid.

10. **Stamina:** This skill might surprise you but chefs need to have an excellent level of physical and mental fitness. Working in a kitchen can be very physically demanding – working long shifts on your feet in hot temperatures and without many breaks is tough. On top of that, the mental energy required to cope with the pressure and be on top of your game, your section, and your kitchen can be huge. An experienced chef will have excellent stamina to remain focused and consistently produce dishes for customers.

> Source: Adapted from Taylor, S. (2019). Top 10 Skills Needed
> to Become a Chef. Available at: www.highspeedtraining.co.uk/
> hub/requirements-to-be-a-chef/

In addition to the proposed balanced culinary competencies framework that reflects on existing literature and responds to current, and especially future occupational and industry demands, it is important to introduce the notion of career-pathing. Closely associated with the traditional principles of the career ladder (vertical moves), career-pathing provides individuals more alternatives, e.g., horizontal career paths (i.e., career lattices), dual career ladders, etc. By espousing the notion that, for a variety of socio-economic reasons, not all individuals want or are able to reach the top of their profession, a reality also due to the paucity of available positions, it is important to identify the competencies that will enable career advancement strategies beyond the traditional vertical moves. Culinary stakeholders must entrust innovative career advancement strategies that also capitalise on horizontal paths, especially as the operational specificities of this industry enable such moves.

Conclusion

Culinary professions require a fine balance between the art of gastronomy, mostly associated with technical aspects, human, and managerial/leadership/entrepreneurial skills. The industry requires well-rounded professionals that possess the ideal KSAs and the proper culinary aptitude and attitude to perform day-to-day operations and guide the sector further into the 21st century. The idea is not just to prepare individuals to find a job, but rather to nurture culinary personas that will elevate their craft via entrepreneurial initiatives, sustainable practices, cultural sensitivity, innovative business growth and internalisation strategies, e-marketing, and the use of social media. The advantages of such a quest are twofold: first to generate jobs for others, and second to elevate the social status and prestige of the professions in the culinary field. From humble beginnings as a refuge for the historically disenfranchised serving the dominant social classes, to their notorious "back of the house" confinement, culinary professionals must now redefine their art, expand their entrepreneurial role, and change food culture at a global scale.

The proposed competency framework, despite its inherent limitations, provides guidelines with a multitude of implications for the industry, academia, and those inspired to pursue culinary careers. For the industry, such a tool can assist, amongst others, in recruitment and selection practices, training and development, and succession planning (Suhairom et al., 2019), whereas for academia it can inform curriculum design by redefining – and justifying the necessity of – the balance between technical and other soft KSAs. This is key as presently most tertiary education programmes mostly focus on technical culinary competencies (Hu, 2010). Finally, for individuals inspired to pursue careers in the culinary field, this framework highlights the recommended KSAs necessary for each level of their career development and progression.

6 Gender and diversity issues in commercial kitchens

Introduction

Chapter 6 explores the causes of gender segregation in kitchens and discusses how female chefs have managed to survive in this hostile environment. Working in commercial kitchens was always considered to be a male-dominated occupation. The challenging working conditions and occupational culture are the key challenges for women in the pursuit of a career in commercial kitchens. The latest developments, such as the #metoo movement, bring to the surface phenomena such as sexual harassment and the wider gender segregation in commercial kitchens. At the same time, however, discrimination issues are also discussed from #blacklivesmatter

DOI: 10.4324/9781003160250-6

actions and the movement, which are also evident in commercial kitchens. There is a paucity of academic studies on gender and ethnic segregation in professional cooking, areas that are explored in this chapter and provide an overview of the key challenges faced by women in kitchens.

Introduction to gender

A diffuse set of meanings has been used to study the concept of gender. In the beginning, the concept of gender referred to the differences between men and women (Connell, 2009), without any separation from sex (Davis et al., 2006), although sex and gender should be differentiated, as explained further. This chapter focuses on gender and how it impacts women's position in commercial kitchens. Gender is a symbol that embodies biological differences in culture as it is socially constructed (Gherardi, 1994). People are born with a sex, but acquire their gender through their social lives and gender roles (Connell, 2009).

Many definitions of gender have been provided, i.e., Acker (1992, p. 566) defined gender as:

> a process by which human activities, practices and social structures are ordered in terms of differentiations between women and men, then an understanding of institutions as "gendered" becomes defined as gender being present within processes, practices, images, ideologies, and distributions of power in the institution.

Gherardi (1994, p. 595) proposed that "in other words, gender is something we think, something we do, and something we make accountable to others". Gender refers to the social roles and expectations from people, as people choose to construct their behaviour and body depending on the situation and context (Gherardi, 1994). Rather than there being a singular femininity or masculinity fixed to the female or male body, respectively, there are a range of femininities and masculinities that are historically, socially, and culturally specific, fluid, and changing (Marinakou, 2012). Pini (2005) proposed that there are dominant, privileged, and hegemonic ways of doing gender in specific sites and times, hence the context where gender is illustrated impacts on people's behaviour. Gender identity is created and negotiated through social interaction and linguistic acts, social rituals, symbols, and practices, which are abundant in commercial kitchens (Cooper et al., 2017).

Gender in organisations

Gender is a key organisational principle, keeping some people (mainly women) in their place and constraining the behaviour of both men and women (Wilson

& Iles, 1996). Studies claiming that gender is irrelevant at work, that workers have no gender, and that jobs are de-embodied are rejected by various studies (i.e., Albors-Garrigos et al., 2020; Marinakou, 2012; Martin, 2006). The experience of both genders at work is influenced by gender roles in organisations and how people acquire and produce symbols, beliefs, and patterns of behaviour within these organisations (Gherardi & Poggio, 2001). Gender impacts on rules, values, and meanings of organisational culture. Gender in organisations reflects the socially constructed image of maleness and femaleness, and specifies any power relations among them (Cano, 2019). For example, Carli (2001) suggested that women who enter traditional male organisational cultures, such as commercial kitchens, are faced with rules assuming that there is a traditional male position and domination. In such competitive work environments as commercial kitchens, "dominant cohorts discriminate their subordinate groups by creating organisational structures to preserve or enhance their privileged position" (Albors-Garrigos et al., 2020, p. 1).

Gender roles in organisations determine how individuals will interact, who will dominate the group, and define any gender differences. Martin (2006) proposed that if people believe that gender matters, then they will behave according to the gender roles ascribed to their gender, and they will interpret this with routinised engagements in verbal and body actions and interactions. Kitchens are thought to be male dominated, supporting the ideology that occupations are gendered. Behaviours in this context are linked to the notions of masculinity and femininity, demonstrating similarities to those in the case of the military (Acker, 1992), a setting which has often been compared to the structure and operation of commercial kitchens, as described in Chapter 1. More specifically, Mennell (1996, p. 23) suggested that "influence of the military model on the realm of professional cooking may also have contributed to the development of a gender-based culinary hierarchy, whilst permeating the occupational identity and culture of chefs". Butler (1990) proposed that as individuals learn from society's expectations, they find females to be nurturers who belong to the kitchen, whereas males are the providers, thus making them the chef in the kitchen who is taught to dominate the field, i.e., culinary arts or gastronomy. For example, exhibition of masculinity in the kitchen includes attaching the knives to the belt (Gonzalez, 2019). Interestingly, as gender roles are linked to everyday practices, society may assume that if females become successful chefs, then they have probably failed at femininity (Butler, 1990).

Gender stereotypes are reproduced in organisations. Such stereotypes support men as being more productive, better leaders, and having greater commitment to work (Marinakou, 2012). Women, in this case, are considered to be physically incapable of dealing with tasks in the kitchen, and are poor leaders with a lack of business skills (Cooper, 1998). Such beliefs support the views that "being a chef remains as 'men's work' and makes it difficult for women to advance within traditional kitchen hierarchies" (Harris & Giuffre, 2015, p. 12). Women sometimes perform masculinity, trying to prove that they are tough in the kitchen, "making femininity a mask that resolves the masculine identification" (Cano, 2019, p. 3). Supporting male domination in kitchens, successful chefs create a brand of their names, and get to be privileged, internalising gender inequality and how men and women identify themselves within the kitchen arena. One's gender exercises control over the other, reinforcing social hierarchies (Bourdieu, 2001). Abarca (2006) claimed that women are usually in a state of "being" in the kitchen, whereas men are in a state of creating, of changing, and of "becoming". Herkes and Redden (2017) similarly propose that men have greater liberty to choose to lead kitchens, whereas women usually serve food and are excluded from leadership positions.

Gender segregation in commercial kitchens settings

The nature of work remains significantly gender-specific, with clear evidence of clusters (of men and women) and gender stereotypes in both mature and emerging economies. Historians propose that cooking is an art and a profession that has been dominated by men (Swinbank, 2002). Dinakaran (2018) supports the view that professional kitchens have been dominated by men since the 14th and 15th centuries, even until the second half of the 20th century. Despite women's involvement in cooking, they are still underrepresented in professional cooking, and in haute cuisine in particular (Dinakaran, 2015). Current data demonstrates that, although women have progressed in culinary management, they still have "a hard road to being recognized as chefs" (Dinakaran, 2015, p. 2). The professional kitchen has been dominated by men, and only a few women have managed to overcome the barriers and become recognised as chefs.

> We have the first women Executive Chef Iyanthi Gunewardene (1998) at Grand Oriental Hotel in Australia, Susan Wolfla at Mandalay Bay (2005) in Las Vegas, Cristeta Comerford at White House (2005) in Washington, and Suzanne Storms (2006) the first women Executive Chef in the Middle East Region.
>
> (Dinakaran, 2015, p. 2)

Although there is a paucity of academic studies addressing the position of women in professional kitchens (Cooper, 2012), journalistic evidence from both the UK and the US proposes that professional kitchens are still male-dominated settings, providing support to occupational gender segregation, and chauvinistic views continue to prevail. Similarly, Harris and Giuffre (2015) add that there has been little research on professional chefs, despite their popularity and exposure from media.

Stockdale (1991, p. 57) defined *occupational gender segregation* as when "the jobs that women do are different from those done by men (horizontal segregation) and women work at lower levels than men in the occupational hierarchy (vertical segregation)". *Occupational vertical segregation* of women in developed countries has been studied by many (i.e., Davidson & Cooper, 1992; Aitchison et al., 1999). The "gender pyramid" is evident in such cases, as positions for progression are dominated by men. Purcell (1996, p. 20) supported the existence of gender role stereotyping and identified three types of jobs done by women: the "contingently-gendered jobs", in which women do jobs that include a role that is mainly gender-neutral, the "sex-typed jobs", in which roles are sex related, and the "patriarchal practice", in which roles are identified and specified by beliefs and practices that reflect gender attributes.

In *occupational horizontal segregation*, women hold positions such as flight attendants and chambermaids, whereas men are pilots or barmen (Earth Summit, 2002); therefore, there are positions that are dominated by men, and others by women. Women who hold such positions are rarely allowed to progress in the hierarchy and become chefs, and hence choose to leave their career and/or the industry. This behaviour is reinforced by working practices and conditions such as those found in commercial kitchens, i.e., irregular and long working hours.

Burrell et al. (1997, p. 173) and Cooper (2012) found that "the atmosphere in French and UK kitchens was often described as 'masculine' and characterised by vulgar jokes or 'banter'", whilst several of their interviewees "indicated that women found this type of atmosphere unpleasant and that it put them off working in the kitchen". Swinbank (2002) further proposed that a macho culture is evident in kitchens, which leads to macho and misogynist language and behaviour. All this working climate is hostile and intimidating for women. The *haute cuisine* sector and commercial kitchens are therefore found to have a reputation for sexism and segregation (Pratten, 2003a). For example, in the UK context, only a few women are found to lead the kitchens of Michelin-star restaurants (Valenti, 2015). Masculinity refers to ideals such as courage, inner direction, aggression, technological skill, mastery, autonomy, group solidarity, adventure, and physical and mental toughness (Adler, 2017). Donaldson (1993) proposed that hegemonic masculinity (also known as "toxic masculinity") encompasses all these traits, while also holding the power and destroying other social groups in the process; such masculinity has long been valued in a brigade. Bourdain (2000) described in his book *Kitchen Confidential: Adventures in the Culinary Underbelly* his experiences as a young cook, including incidents with drugs, alcohol, and harassment, among others, but he mainly emphasised the physical toughness.

This masculine culture of professional kitchens is one of the reasons for women's exclusion from professional cooking. Cooper (2012) and Swinbank (2002) support this view and add that modern professional kitchens are characterised by hierarchical structure and a male management style similar to that of military-inherited traits. Within this masculine culture, women feel pressured to use sexual favours for advancement opportunities (Kurnaz et al., 2018; Jayaraman, 2016). Studies propose that women who thrived in the industry have adopted traits and behaviours associated with the masculine kitchen culture (Gonzalez, 2019). For example, Arvela (2017) explains that women often embrace the tattoo culture to balance the gender scale and fit in with the masculinisation standards in a kitchen. In order to make it in professional kitchens, Harris and Giuffre (2015) found that female chefs adopted a masculine leadership style, blunt and leading like men, had to be tough, and felt pressure to act like "one of the guys", meaning to be less caring toward staff and customers. Although female chefs adopted a communication style that included yelling, cursing, and making sexualised jokes, they actually stated "we are acting like a chef" (Harris & Giuffre, 2015, p. 137). Male chefs in the same study suggested that sexual joking and teasing was used as a test to determine whether women were tough enough for the kitchen and able to find their position in the team (p. 131). Male chefs continued that women chefs have to manage their emotions, as expressions of frustration, anger, and disappointment expressed through crying were considered signs of women's inability to handle the work of a chef (p. 97).

In contrast to the above discussion, Fine (1987) proposed that it is not gender that is the problem, but rather the cultural traditions surrounding gender stipulating that women have to adopt the occupational culture and masculine behaviours found in kitchens so as not to be considered a threat to the team. Men are not misogynists; they just want to avoid disruptions to "the patterns of male interaction which most contribute to building group solidarity and belongingness" (p. 144). He added that women could be accepted by their male counterparts, as long as they accepted and adopted patterns of male behaviours and bonding. He emphasised that the male and female cooks'/chefs' relationship only connects with women's attitudes and how they will behave in the kitchen. In this setting, norms and rules are difficult, if not unlikely, to change rapidly; hence, women should comply and, if possible, accept them. In reference to disruptions, some women chefs reported that they were also criticised for their appearance, for being too attractive, and that appearance was a metric for whether they fit in (or not) in the kitchen (p. 105). Nevertheless, more recent studies suggest that female chefs have ignored the harassment that is pertinent in commercial kitchens and they "avoid feeling victimized" (Gonzalez, 2019, p. 65). Successful female chefs concentrate on work, trying to balance work with their personal life to achieve and maintain success (Haddaji et al., 2017), and disregard occupational gender segregation in commercial kitchens. Ferguson (2007) suggested that female chefs are quieter, leading to debates about whether they behave in a masculine manner to be accepted in the kitchen or they follow this profession because of their personal characteristics and traits. Studies confirm that women chefs adopt gender neutrality to demonstrate that gender does not necessarily shape their career outcomes (Harris & Giuffre, 2015, p. 128). Moreover, Cairns and Johnston (2015) suggest that women are more involved with food security projects, and men with food policy projects, which delineates what is acceptable in Westernised society. This view demonstrates the domination of male leaders, requiring further progressive efforts to be made in supporting women's progression in the food industry (Figure 6.1).

The glass ceiling and working conditions in commercial kitchens

Today's hospitality and tourism environment is characterised by uncertainty and unpredictability. Challenges such as Brexit in the UK, the COVID-19 pandemic, and shortage of skills in the culinary arts add to the challenges women face in commercial kitchens' employment (Kurnaz et al., 2018). According to the Office of National Statistics (2018), there are a total of 250,000

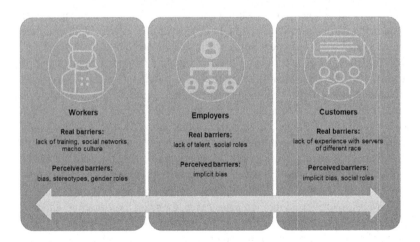

Figure 6.1 Barriers and occupational segregation in commercial kitchens

professional chefs in the UK, but only 18.5% (some 46,000) are women. The Bureau of Labor Statistics (2021) states that there are 148,000 chefs and head cooks in the US, but only 19% of them are women. Similarly, Kurnaz et al. (2018, p. 120) state that in "Sweden, 66% of executive chefs consist of men". More importantly, there are very few women with Michelin stars, and even less have claimed three Michelin stars. The first to achieve a Michelin star were Eugenie Brazier and Marie Bourgeois in 1933, and Margeurite Bise in 1951 (Cole, 2019). Other female chefs have followed, but still remain few in number among the 130 chefs with Michelin stars worldwide, making up less than 4% of the three-Michelin-starred restaurant population.

Banner (1973, p. 212) argued that

> there have been no female great chefs throughout the ages "because the role has not been available to them", despite women's continuous involvement in the creation of new dishes and new cuisines as part of everyday cooking, and their indirect influence on male professional chefs.

He added that men excluded women in order to reduce competition and maintain the status of their profession in the world's eyes, which was a result of the sexual division of labour in culinary arts (Swinbank, 2002). In male-dominated occupations, women face barriers related to hegemonic masculinity which prevent them from rising higher in the hierarchy. These invisible barriers are part of what is known as the "glass ceiling" phenomenon, which refers to barriers for minorities as well (Wilson, 2014). There is very little research on the glass ceiling in the food industry, but key barriers have been identified (Andilolo & Ranteallo, 2016). The glass ceiling barriers include lack of mentoring, lack of managerial-leadership experience, exclusion from informal networks (old boys club), and gender stereotypes (Winn, 2004); women have traditionally been excluded from professional circles (Haddaji et al., 2017) and also have to put up with jokes, pressure to adapt to the macho atmosphere, and deal with harassment (Kurnaz et al., 2018). Many women quit their jobs due to work-life imbalance, lack of respect, and harassment. For example, Andilolo and Ranteallo (2016, p. 7) present the case of a pastry chef who filed a complaint against three senior chefs: "she was verbally harassed and routinely had her breasts and crotch touched at work, among other indignities". Many other examples are found to describe the sexual abusive behaviours in kitchens which harm women; surprisingly (and sadly), they are covered up through the culinary structure and culture of secrecy.

Other barriers include long working hours that create conflict between work and family, mainly affecting female chefs who are reported to follow one of the three choices between leaving the kitchen for another job, delaying childbearing, or choosing and/or adapting roles between work or family to make them more compatible (Kurnaz et al., 2018). Work in commercial kitchens includes working late at night, over weekends and holidays, thus demotivating women from pursuing a career as a chef due to family obligations. Harris and Giuffre (2015, p. 167) propose that female participants in their study "left kitchen work as it was incompatible with family needs" and continued that "schedules and work conditions that may be considered acceptable at first may become unacceptable after having children", "restaurant kitchen work is also characterized by a lack of health benefits". Other reasons include physical strength and stamina required to do the job, as it entails "lifting heavy pots or standing on one's feet for fifteen to eighteen hours a day" (Harris & Giuffre, 2015, p. 91). As already discussed in Chapter 3, chefs have to change jobs in order to maximise their career outcomes and "accumulate as much human, social and cultural capital as possible"; hence, it is difficult for female chefs to move often if they have family obligations (p. 91). As few women are found at the top of the hierarchy in kitchens, even fewer have become mentors to support and encourage younger females to enter into the profession or stay in kitchen work.

Diversity and discrimination in kitchen settings

Power impacts on those who are most marginalised in society, such as those influenced by class, race, sexual orientation, disability, and gender (Collins & Bilge, 2016). The kitchen is a social institution with evidence of social injustice through violation of the basic rights for those who are usually at the bottom of the hierarchy. Numbers propose that there is discrimination in commercial kitchens. Krogstad et al. (2018) claim that there are more than seven million unauthorised immigrants working in the US. Since they are illegal, they prefer not to report any violations; thus, those cooks, chefs, and dishwashers are having their main rights violated with improper remuneration. When analysing masculinity in the kitchen, a male privilege for immigrant chefs is still evident, but they also face other sources of oppression (Bourdieu, 1996). Different movements demonstrate the existence of discrimination, injustice, and exploitation in the foodservices industry; movements such as #metoo or #blacklivesmatter. Professional kitchens are a white man's world in which ethnic minorities and women are usually excluded (Krogstad et al., 2018).

Consequently, the structures of unconscious socialisation are uncovered, where segregation becomes interconnected with gender and race, and the pay gap becomes a normalised issue. The pay gap is giving higher status to men, as they make 30% more than their female colleagues do. There are still wage differences in male and female managerial jobs, as usually women are occupied with jobs in lower-paying areas of a company's operations (Marinakou, 2012). As previously discussed, gender segregation is found to be an explanation

Figure 6.2 Pay gap between male and female chefs in the US. Source: adapted from ROC (2015)

of the pay gap between genders (Harris & Giuffre, 2015). The Restaurant Opportunities Centers (ROC) report (2015) presented examples of pay among chefs in California, claiming that there is an average of 7% difference in pay between male and female chefs, as shown in Figure 6.2.

The main challenge women face seems to be the slow progress into leadership positions, which suggests discrimination, especially where the most power is being exercised. Although research suggests that the recruitment, full development, and retention of qualified women is increasingly recognised as being essential to the economic survival of businesses, women are still underrepresented in commercial kitchens (Albors-Garrigos et al., 2020).

#Metoo has become an international movement against sexual harassment and assault, mainly in the workplace. Khomami (2017) emphasises the attention to power imbalances between men and women creating unsafe and unhealthy work environments for those with less power, i.e., women in kitchens. Many women came out of secrecy and spoke about sexual harassment and abuse in restaurants. Chefs were named and shamed, which led to some cases of restaurant closures, as owners did not want to be associated with the perpetrators (Gonzalez, 2019). The #metoo movement shed light on health issues in the brigade, such as substance abuse, which may bring about sexual abuse. "The hierarchy of the brigade makes coercion more possible than it might be in more egalitarian workplaces" (Gonzalez, 2019,

p. 63). The movement also referred to "limited opportunities for advancement for females who are more vulnerable to pressures from superiors that are gatekeepers for their professional advancement" (p. 64).

The 2020 movement for Black lives, #blacklivesmatter (BLM), set off by the murder of George Floyd, has rippled through a variety of industries, including that of restaurants and commercial kitchens. The ROC reported that in the US in 2015, Black workers earned lower wages than others did in all occupations and positions. Interestingly, they are left out of fine dining and are over-represented in fast food chains. Furthermore, the mobility of workers of colour is limited, as they have been denied promotion, and despite their adjustment for education and language proficiency, receive 56% lower earnings when compared to equally qualified white workers. The movement urged for scrutiny on the discrimination endemic to the restaurant and foodservice industry.

The findings of the ROC (2015) report propose that structural barriers are the cause of inequality in the restaurant industry. People of colour are more likely to experience higher unemployment levels, lower quality education and housing, and reduced health outcomes, "leading to lower economic opportunities, weaker social networks, and reduced chances of economic mobility" (p. 20). Implicit bias, the subconscious attitudes and stereotypes, are also discussed in the report; "implicit bias affects behaviours and intentions, such that even though employers state they are not racist or aim to have a diverse staff, it can ultimately lead to inhibition of fair hiring, promotion, and working processes" (p. 22). This bias was demonstrated in the demographic composition of restaurants, as most owners took pride in the diversity in their restaurants, yet they had more segregation between service and kitchen positions. Interestingly, such movements have changed behaviours in commercial kitchens. For example, Bourdain (2004) stated that he regrets supporting the "bro-culture" in the kitchen. He became an advocate for women and immigrants, and supports a more refined kitchen culture (Gonzalez, 2019).

Nowadays, the pandemic has made the future of restaurants even more uncertain. Furloughs and layoffs made the most marginalised employees more vulnerable, with an explosion of all kinds of abuse. Regardless of the situation and crises, active policy changes and vehicles for accountability across the industry should be created to eliminate discrimination in commercial kitchens, as well.

Women in commercial kitchens – success factors

The previous discussion provides an overview of gender issues and challenges in commercial kitchens. Women face a variety of barriers to progress in the hierarchy ladder in the chef occupation, and become accepted as valued members of the team. The foodservices sector has been male dominated for a very long time, making it difficult for women to enter this work context in which women are seen as invaders who have to prove that they belong in the team/brigade. Notably, representation of women in kitchens has been growing. The National Restaurant Association (2016) in the US proposes that the number of female-owned restaurants has grown by 40% in the last ten years, presenting entrepreneurship as a solution to toxic kitchen culture. Female chefs have found ways to overcome the barriers and break the glass ceiling by either setting up their own businesses, where they use their own preferred leadership and management style (Adler, 2017), or "talk more about how they manage their kitchens differently offering more flexibility, support, creating spaces more inclusive of a range of genders, sexualities, and ethnicities reducing violence" (Harris & Giuffre, 2015, p. 128). Sexual harassment and assaults are still rife in some countries like France, even two years after the #metoo movement, but efforts are being made by the government to change perceptions and working conditions in the sector (Valenti, 2019).

Many female chefs managed to become established in professional kitchens and develop a reputation and a brand of their own. In order to accomplish this, they followed certain strategies and behaviours, which are further discussed. Women are influenced by their mentors, and have personalised their style to their own personalities and traits. Women sought support and guidance from mentors in their initial career stages (Haddaji et al., 2017). For women chefs, managing, training, and delegating are essential for the restaurant's success and becoming an excellent chef. In their study, Haddaji et al. (2017, p. 334) found that "adopting a feminine style in managing their restaurant (women) was not considered a constraint in the kitchen workplace". Women seek public recognition by marketing themselves and using their gender as a positive factor (Harris & Giuffre, 2015). Haddaji et al. (2017, p. 324) propose that female chefs have followed approaches such as "social activism, entrepreneurship, working with celebrity chefs and getting support from experts". Valenti (2019) confirms this view and states that "to eliminate sexism from the kitchen, women chefs just start their own". Moreover, to remain in the profession, female chefs are motivated and driven by their need to learn to enhance their knowledge and skills in order to evolve to the top of their industry. They have "passion for food, for gastronomy and the kitchen" (Haddaji et al., 2017, p. 334; Harris & Giuffre, 2015).

Some choose to delay having (or not to have) children to instead concentrate on their career, while others have managed to progress in their occupation with the support of the family. Women chefs have found support in businesses (usually owned by other women) that offer flexibility and are family-oriented (Valenti, 2019). Women chefs propose that restaurant owners should embrace diversity and make kitchens more hospitable to women by adopting a zero-tolerance harassment policy, breaking up the boys club and closing the pay gap. Female chefs suggest putting women and women of colour into leadership positions to support equal opportunities, as well as offering mentorships and apprenticeships (Hartke, 2018). There are associations that promote such initiatives of mentoring opportunities for women, i.e., the Women Chefs and Restauranteurs (WCR), the James Beard Foundation, and Les Dames d' Escoffier (Hartke, 2018).

Management of a professional kitchen should (and must) implement a code of behaviour in the workplace that creates a safe environment for both men and women (Gonzalez, 2019). Other initiatives include a variety of equal opportunities policies and/or practices; for example, better recognition of unpaid work and rebalance pay between men and women. Family-friendly policies including flexible work schedules could be the norm in commercial kitchens. Performance appraisals should ensure fairness and transparency. Other measures could promote entrepreneurship among women with the aid of financial and training programmes. Gender diversity and gender equality could be promoted and supported, eliminating bias in recruitment in the foodservices industry.

BOX 6.1 SUCCESS FACTORS FOR FEMALE CHEFS

Chef Maria Loi is regarded as one of the world's best chefs, with count-less accolades to her name (Vora, 2020). She's the Executive Chef of Loi Estiatorio (a Greek casual fine dining restaurant) in New York and the author of over 30 cookbooks, including the official cookbook of the Athens 2004 Olympic Games. Chef Loi's famous patrons include for-mer President Obama and at the time Vice President Biden in the White House in 2012. During the COVID-19 pandemic she delivered thousands of meals to hospitals around New York City. She is also involved with the Harvard TH Chan School of Public Health and the Culinary Institute of America regarding the powerful health benefits of *The Greek Diet*, focus-ing on healthy, balanced eating and wellbeing. Below she identifies the key ingredients to survive and prosper in commercial kitchens:

"To be successful in this industry, not only as a woman, but in general, you must never give up. Determination, passion, and dedica-tion to the craft are important, however, it is also crucial to share your knowledge, no matter what position you hold. I have learned so many things from every rung of the brigade system, and from all different cultures and walks of life in the kitchen. The key is to be open minded with an open heart – but, remember to be strong, focus, and hold firm to what you believe."

Source: Loi (2021, email communication)

Women chefs care more about feelings and are more empathetic than men, making them more efficient and effective leaders. Although male chefs lead by example, following masculine norms and command of authority, female chefs are more transformational in their leadership style (Marinakou & Giousmpasoglou, 2019). They have started supporting and mentoring other females who enter into the industry, creating a culture that does not make it "into a male-female thing" (Valenti, 2019). Focusing on relationships with the cooks in the kitchen, as well as on culture and team building, may bring about change to the industry and adopt a management and leadership style that women chefs use (Krishna, 2017). Chef Daniella Soto-Innes in New York plays upbeat music in the kitchen before service starts. "She goes to yoga and spin classes before work and makes sure to get enough sleep and fill her meals with vegetables". "She is an advocate for fair pay and rejects the traditional hierarchy, refusing to take sole credit for her success and the success of her restaurants" (Gonzalez, 2019, p. 66). Restaurant owners should recognise that women have different needs, which should be accom-modated at the workplace. They should accept that women manage differ-ently and have different attitudes than men in the workplace, but are equally

Table 6.1 Barriers and facilitators for women in commercial kitchens

BARRIERS	FACILITATORS

WORKPLACE CULTURE

• Masculinity – macho behaviour	• Resilience & determination
• Bullying and violence	• Consistency
• Harassment	• Women's patience and endurance
• Competitiveness	• Report abuse and harassment
• Physical endurance and strength	• Determination, ambition
• Lack of opportunities for female chefs	• It does not make a difference attitude
	• Positive organisational culture to support women's style
	• Embrace diversity
	• Equal opportunities initiatives
	• Family-friendly policies
	• Training opportunities

SOCIAL ROLES – GENDER ROLES AND STEREOTYPES

• Nurturing role	• Maintain this style
• Work-life imbalance – personal investment	• Work-life balance policies
	• Family-friendly policies

LEADERSHIP

• Lack of mentors	• Mentoring other female chefs
• Adopt masculine leadership styles (authoritarian) – strong personality/aggressive	• Adopt a more feminine style, personalise it
• Moving – changing jobs	• Self-employment
	• Develop their own brand

WORKING CONDITIONS

• Long working hours	• Work structure and schedule
• Pay gap	• Equal pay

effective. The above points about women's positions in the workplace are illustrated in Table 6.1.

Conclusions

We have indeed come a long way from the notion that a woman's place is in the domestic kitchen, and that the only kitchen appropriate for a man is the professional one. Women have to work hard to be accepted as chefs, but evidence suggests that both men and women experience harsh working conditions and atmosphere on their way up. Commercial kitchens are male-dominated settings, making experiences unique for women and other minority groups, thus providing evidence of gender and race discrimination. History of the chefs' occupation, culture, gender stereotypes, and women's descriptions of their experiences all enhance the perception of masculinity in commercial kitchens.

There are a number of factors that hinder women's advancement in the restaurant business. Discriminatory policies in the organisational culture of commercial kitchens, informal and cultural forms of discrimination are some of the factors identified in this study. A number of barriers have been identified that justify the number of women who enter (and remain in) professional kitchens, such as the working conditions and the macho ethos, which is unpleasant and intimidating for women to fit into. Female chefs should be prepared to embrace the occupational culture by enriching the culture of the occupation with the inclusion of feminine management and leadership styles. Success is based on personal attributes, skills, hard work, and dedication to their occupation. Although traditional, stereotypical notions that women are not tough enough to handle the challenging environment of commercial kitchens persist, there is evidence of progress through the substantial number of successful women chefs, some of whom interestingly report that the "doors are open for women", despite the evidence of gender segregation and discrimination.

7 Kitchen deviance – Banter, bullying, and violence

Introduction

The popular interest in commercial kitchen life through the phenomenon of celebrity chefs has grown considerably over the past two decades in both sides of the Atlantic and more recently in the rest of the world. In this chapter we explore the "dark side" of kitchens brigades; more specifically we investigate the phenomena of banter, bullying, and violence in commercial kitchens (Box 7.1). The glamourised image of the "macho, creative and violent" chef does not reflect by any means the working conditions in this profession. Based on the anecdotal stories provided by Burrow et al. (2015), this demanding working environment would be better described as "heaven and hell" for the junior chefs aspiring to run their own kitchen one day. In this context, the banter and bullying phenomena have been for a

DOI: 10.4324/9781003160250-7

long time part of chefs' occupational culture (Giousmpasoglou et al., 2018). Although not necessarily accepted by its members they have been used (and continue to be) as a means of induction, occupational socialisation, and motivation in commercial kitchens with questionable results (Bloisi & Hoel, 2008). On the other hand, empirical findings suggest that banter and bullying behaviours have no effect on either job satisfaction or commitment (Alexander et al., 2012). In other words, the existing research suggests that although bullying is generally regarded as a contemptuous behaviour both by academics and practitioners, it is a standard informal practice used to achieve high-performance standards, especially in Michelin-starred kitchen brigades (Giousmpasoglou et al., 2018). This chapter investigates the effect of banter, bullying, and violence in kitchen brigades. In addition, the chapter explores the relationship between young chefs' occupational socialisation with deviant behaviour such as bullying and violence.

BOX 7.1 KITCHEN CONFIDENTIAL

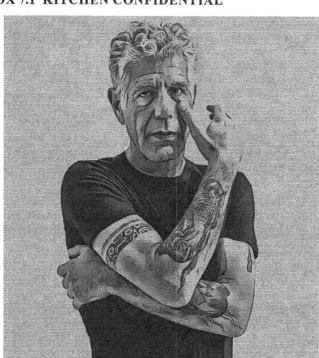

In his autobiographical novel *Kitchen Confidential*, New York chef Anthony Bourdain (2000) presents a detailed and vivid account of "kitchen life" from an insider's point of view. Despite the flourishing trend for chef biographies and other written accounts of both high-profile chefs and kitchen life, *Kitchen Confidential* is unique in that it provides a particularly insightful depiction of the culture of professional cooking, whilst pointing to the importance of the kitchen environment in terms of understanding the identity of chefs. This kitchen environment is depicted in crude terms as a testosterone-heavy, male-dominated world, made up of individuals who find themselves on the fringe of society and running away from something in their life, or in Bourdain's (2000, p. 61) words, "wacked-out moral degenerates, dope fiends, refugees, a thuggish assortment of drunks, sneak thieves, sluts and psychopaths". Indeed, in his later work, Bourdain (2010, pp. 57–58) goes on to further argue that:

> Smoking weed at the end of the day is nearly always a good idea ... Treating despair with drugs and alcohol is a time-honoured tradition ... if you look around you at the people you work with, many of them are – or will eventually be – alcoholics and drug abusers.

Besides, for Bourdain (2000, p. 124), chefs share a peculiar world-view, together with unusual customs, rituals, and practices that define them as a "tribe". Their unsocial working hours indeed contribute to their exclusion of "normal" social interaction and their subsequent deep commitment to their colleagues, or what Bourdain (2000, p. 56) refers to as a "blind, near-fanatical loyalty ... under battlefield conditions". Furthermore, according to Bourdain (2010, p. 209), "the kitchen is the last meritocracy". He pointedly remarks that:

> Male, female, gay, straight, legal, illegal, country of origin – who cares? You can either cook an omelet or you can't. ... There's no lying in the kitchen. The restaurant kitchen may indeed be the last, glorious meritocracy – where anybody with the skills and the heart is welcomed.
>
> *(pp. 53–54)*

In addition, Bourdain illustrates the sense of communal solidarity that exists among chefs. Indeed, according to Bourdain (2000, p. 55), a chef "never shows up late, never calls in sick, and works through pain and injury", although it is possible that chefs may actually do so out of awe and respect for the kitchen hierarchy. At the same time, Bourdain (2000, p. 293) presents a harsh portrait of chef culture where new recruits are treated as "cattle", denied a personality, and where verbal insults about an individual's personal circumstances, sexuality, and physical appearance are commonplace. Such examples underpin Bourdain's (2000, p. 3) description of the chef's world as "a culture whose centuries-old militaristic hierarchy and ethos of 'rum, buggery and the lash' make for a mix of unwavering order and nerve-shattering chaos".

Source: adapted from Cooper (2012), pp. 75–76
Image created by the authors

Forms of bullying

The concept of bullying at work relates to persistent exposure of the victim to negative and aggressive behaviours of a psychological nature (Leymann, 1996). These behaviours (Figure 7.1) can be systematically directed to one or more colleagues, with devastating results such as stigmatisation and victimisation of the recipients(s) (Bjorkqvist et al., 1994). As a result, the victims suffer from health problems after some time such as severe psychiatric

Figure 7.1 Forms of bullying at work. Source: adapted from Maggie et al. (2017) and Cheary, (n.d.)

and psychosomatic impairment (Einarsen & Nielsen, 2015), whereas the offenders may not be affected at all (Zapf & Gross, 2001). The nature of behaviours linked to workplace bullying in a commercial kitchen environment involve the exposure of victims to verbal abuse such as offensive remarks, insults, and criticism (Bloisi & Hoel, 2008; Burrow et al., 2015); in a few cases bullying can escalate to physical violence (or threats of such violence), such as throwing kitchen utensils or hot food at the victim/s (Giousmpasoglou et al., 2018; Johns & Menzel, 1999).

The origins of bullying may be better understood with Einarsen's (1999) classification into two main categories/themes, namely predatory and dispute-related bullying. In the first case, the victim is found accidentally in a situation where the offender/predator is demonstrating power or taking advantage of the victim's weakness. Ashforth (1994) calls this a "petty tyranny" and refers to leaders who exercise their power over others through arbitrariness and self-aggrandisement. The UK celebrity chefs Marco Pierre White and Gordon Ramsay are great examples of predatory bullying, with many references in their written accounts and/or TV shows (Mac Con Iomaire, 2008; Midgley, 2005). Cooper (2012) suggests that the intimidatory and violent behaviour and the resultant physical and mental damage caused, and symptoms exhibited, are likened to those of *Battered Child Syndrome*. This refers to injuries sustained by a child as a result of physical abuse usually inflicted by an adult caregiver who can be a parent or custodian (Kempe et al., 1962). The symptoms of poor self-image, anger, rage, anxiety, fear, depression, and substance abuse can all exist in cases of *Battered Child Syndrome* and can also be observed in chefs and members of the kitchen brigade alike who have been subjected to these various psychological and physical bullying techniques. As in cases of children who have suffered abuse, these symptoms can present themselves immediately, or can emerge after a protracted period of time, or may never emerge to a significant degree, dependant on the psychosocial make-up of the individual concerned (Carter, 2015) (Figure 7.2).

On the other hand, "dispute-related" bullying occurs as a result of highly escalated interpersonal conflicts (Einarsen et al., 2011). The difference between workplace bullying and interpersonal conflict lays in the frequency and duration of what is also known as "office wars" (van de Vliert, 1998); such conflicts include intense emotional involvement and the ultimate goal is to eliminate the opponent(s) by attacking each other's self-esteem and self-image. The escalation of this situation will eventually lead one of the parties to a position unable to defend him/herself or retaliate against increasingly aggressive behaviours; the outcome of this situation is the victimisation of the weaker parties (Chirila & Costantin, 2013). In some extreme cases victims commit suicide or consider it seriously as the ultimate solution (Leymann, 1990). In a commercial kitchen context, the

Figure 7.2 The Battered Child Syndrome in commercial kitchens' context

exercise of dispute-related bullying would be limited to a few isolated cases due to the existence of a strong leader (head chef) (Balazs, 2001). In addition, the regimental discipline and the strong ties among the team members leave no room for personal rivalries (Burrow et al., 2015; Cooper, 2012).

Bullying and violence as part of the occupational culture

The partie system introduced in the early 18th century (see Chapter 1) continues to serve as a fundamental building block in the formation of the occupational identity and culture in commercial kitchens (Cooper et al., 2017). It can be argued that one of the implications generated from the use of this traditional work organisation method is the existence of abusive behaviour and more particular bullying. Kitchen bullying and violence became a topical issue in Great Britain during the 1990s following the screening of a few television programmes such as Gordon Ramsay's *Boilling Point* and the *Big Story*, which revealed kitchen life behind the scenes in Michelin-starred restaurants (Mac Con Iomaire, 2008). The popularity of this phenomenon has triggered a stream of research where chefs were chosen as the sole objects of analysis and addressed some specific aspects of their occupational culture, such as bullying and violence (i.e., Alexander et al., 2012; Burrow et al., 2015; Giousmpasoglou et al., 2018; Johns & Menzel, 1999; Murray-Gibbons & Gibbons, 2007).

Johns and Menzel (1999, p. 103) justified chefs' violent and bullying behaviour by highlighting the physical pressures of the job, such as the heat, the noise from machines and shouting voices, the variable demand leading to peaks of activity, and "a sense of constant scrutiny" linked to chefs having to maintain standards of excellence whilst relying on their staff for food production. Yet, further analysis prompts Johns & Menzel to acknowledge that although physical pressures do contribute to kitchen violence, it is the socio-cultural aspects of kitchen work that seem mostly to blame for violence (Hoel & Salin, 2003). The resigned attitude of many of their informants indeed seems to illustrate the extent to which kitchen violence has become deeply embedded in chefs' working culture. Midgley (2005) confirms Johns and Menzel's (1999) claims by drawing upon informal observational research undertaken in a Glaswegian French restaurant by Phil Hodgson of Ashridge Business School, according to whom the persistence of a macho culture can be attributed to chefs passing on learned behaviour. He (ibid., p. 53) also acknowledges the scope of the bullying problem in the industry and its likely consequences:

> Catering is a notoriously tough business with high stress levels. When bullying is stirred into the mix, disaster can be the result, even for those who consider themselves psychologically robust. One of the results of a military style of management in the kitchens is that catering is an industry riven by poor health and high levels of drug abuse and alcoholism.

Such comments may indeed help perpetuate the myth that kitchen violence is part of the work environment, by converting it into an "external enemy" (Johns & Menzel, 1999, p. 107) and therefore shifting the onus/blame away from individuals. Despite his lack of empirical data, Wood (2000) similarly argues that the deeply ingrained stereotype of the creative, temperamental, and volatile chef may in fact merely facilitate or allow chefs to behave in this way, since creativity may be used to explain or excuse bullying, temperament, and volatility.

The prevalence of bullying and harassment in professional kitchens has also been confirmed through quantitative means by Murray-Gibbons and Gibbons (2007) in a survey with 40 chefs in Northern Ireland, by Mathisen et al. (2008) in a survey of 207 employees in 70 Norwegian restaurants, and more recently by Alexander et al. (2012) in a survey with 164 chefs in Scotland. All three studies indeed provide evidence to suggest that primary sources of occupational stress not only include excessive workload and communication issues with management, but also experiences of bullying and harassment. Drawing upon Johns and Menzel's (1999) myths of kitchen violence, both Murray-Gibbons and Gibbons (2007) and Mathisen et al. (2008) respectively argue that such aggressive behaviour is often seen as the norm of the kitchen and that head chefs and managers should therefore nurture a more supportive working environment in order to prevent threats of violence and challenge such kitchen norms.

The role of bullying and violence in occupational socialisation

The creation and maintenance of the regimental environment in kitchen brigades goes through the employment of what is described as "kitchen banter". Banter and bullying are deeply embedded in the partie system and chefs' occupational culture. Giousmpasoglou et al. (2018) found that the friendly banter, verbal insults, teasing and mockery, and practical jokes and pranks that go on in the kitchen between members of the kitchen brigade are part and parcel of the everyday routine of "kitchen life" (Alexander et al., 2012). Cooper (2012) suggests that the limits between banter and bullying are not always clearly defined. The abuse of kitchen banter on behalf of the head chef and the use of predatory bullying practices are persistent phenomena in kitchen life.

Midgley (2005) highlights the tendency of high-profile chefs, such as Gordon Ramsay and Anthony Bourdain, to proudly recount stories of how they were bullied as a trainee, whilst asserting the necessity to run a kitchen in an aggressive manner to maintain discipline and achieve results. Further evidence can also be found in the following quote from chef Marco Pierre White (1990, p. 12), which is a particularly striking illustration of Johns and Menzel's (1999) claims that kitchen violence and bullying is regarded as a necessary part of cooks' training by the victims themselves:

> The boys in my team know that if they want to get to the top they've got to take the shit. Harveys [White's former restaurant] is the hardest kitchen in Britain; it's the SAS of kitchens. But you don't get to the top by being pampered.

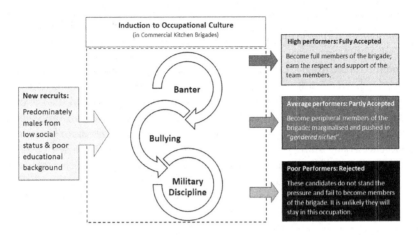

Figure 7.3 The induction and occupational socialisation process for chefs

The use of banter and bullying is the main vehicle for the junior chefs' induction, and occupational socialisation (Figure 7.3) in kitchen brigades (Giousmpasoglou et al., 2018). The use of both kitchen banter and predatory bullying serve several functions. As well as being used to motivate members of the kitchen brigade and to maintain discipline, order, authority, and control, it is a means of letting off steam and a way of initiating new recruits (Johns & Menzel, 1999). Part of this initiation may involve what can be termed initiation rites, in other words, practical jokes or pranks, mainly at the expense of young trainees. Indeed, such rites or rituals serve to reinforce the social ties, the bonds between individuals; they also constitute a way of testing new recruits before accepting them as a member of the group.

Giousmpasoglou et al. (2018) also confirm the relationship between the use of banter and bullying and the new members' performance. It can be thus argued that kitchen banter and bullying also serve to exclude less physically and mentally robust members of the kitchen brigade. It would appear that given the difficulty of the job, both physically and mentally, members of the kitchen brigade tend to pursue such social customs and practices as part of a common group effort to put newcomers to the test in order to prove their worth and weed out the new recruits who are unlikely to commit to the job and fit in and become accepted as part of the team (Pratten, 2003a).

Research in occupational socialisation also suggests that there are certain occupational groups such as nurses (Quine, 2001), military and paramilitary professionals (Archer, 1999), and chefs (Alexander et al., 2012) who accept bullying as a means of induction in their occupational culture; those who survive the enduring harsh treatment from the older group members earn the right to be part of the group. Alexander et al. (2012, p. 1253) suggest that "aggression, violence and humiliation facilitate the banter that allows chefs to bond and be sure that everyone is capable of dealing with the pressure of service". As such, it is argued that bullying and violence are directly linked with the process of the new chefs' occupational socialisation and induction to the occupational culture.

In both the catering industry and the military, the same notions exists of "building" a functioning member of a unit by means of the initial removal of their previous behaviour patterns, followed by the subsequent rebuilding of these behaviour patterns to conform to those required by the organisation (Salin & Hoel, 2011). In this way, both in the catering industry and in the military, once they have been through this process, an individual can be relied on to perform the correct actions in the correct manner at the correct time, to a far higher degree than individuals who have not endured this type of induction. The aggressive and violent nature of induction into the catering industry for young, new recruits is shown here as being the result of imitation on the part of more senior, higher-ranking chefs – these chefs in turn imitating the behaviour learnt from and handed down by their superiors during their time as new recruits (Alexander et al., 2012). In Cooper's (2012) study, the majority of the chefs reported that receiving abuse as a junior chef and then reversing the roles as a chef is part of the socialisation process that builds up the "macho" character needed to survive in a commercial kitchen:

> You knock them down and build them up, then knock them down and build them up. I have had it done a lot – a lot. The Anonymous was a prime example. I got ridden for about six months by the senior sous-chef. … He rode me every day – every day. But that's the way it was then.
>
> (Cooper et al., 2017, p. 1372)

Those who cannot cope with the constant pressure either leave or are pushed to what Crompton and Sanderson (1986) call "gendered niches" such as the salads or the pastry section (Burrow et al., 2015). The above findings suggest a link between banter and socialisation at work; in this context banter is used to determine the ability of the young chefs to cope with the environment and the high job demands (Alexander et al., 2012).

Conclusion

This chapter provided useful insights to the role of banter, bullying, and violence in kitchen brigades, especially during the new members' occupational socialisation phase. The starting point in our effort to understand the existence of this phenomenon is the centuries-old militaristic hierarchy that characterises the occupational culture of chefs is deeply embedded in kitchen culture and the rigidly hierarchical nature of the kitchen brigade (Salin & Hoel, 2011). In addition, the low occupational status in countries such as the US, Great Britain, and Ireland that prevailed for centuries until the advent of *haute cuisine* and celebrity chefs further reinforces the existence of the *partie system* (see also Chapter 1). According to Cooper (2012), while the formal hierarchy of the *partie* system may be more flexible than in previous decades, the militaristic hierarchy of the kitchen brigade is still, albeit to a lesser extent, prevalent in today's kitchens, as there is a need for structure and discipline in order to maintain order, authority, and control. As previously highlighted, these are requirements due to the intense nature of the job and the extreme working environment (i.e., consistently executing each and every dish to an exact standard of quality and excellence day in, day out, under severe temporal constraints, in a highly pressurised and stressful environment). Hence, such military organisation and the highly regimented nature of the kitchen brigade are understood by all the members of the kitchen brigade as a *sine qua non* in the kitchen, something that keeps them performing as a team in order to ultimately and of paramount importance consistently achieve and maintain a standing of quality and excellence day in, day out.

8 AOD use and coping with stress

Introduction

Several empirical studies on alcohol and other drug (AOD) use in various occupational groups have been contacted in the hospitality context (i.e., Belhassen & Shani, 2012; Pizam, 2010); nevertheless, little research has been carried out on the role of AOD use in the working life of chefs. According to Anderson (1998), the term substance abuse is commonly used to refer to an overindulgence and/or dependence on a substance, including alcohol, stimulants such as crack, cocaine, methamphetamine, hallucinogens, marijuana, and opioids (Table 8.1). Substance abuse also includes the misuse of prescription medications obtained illegally, such as morphine

DOI: 10.4324/9781003160250-8

Table 8.1 Classification of AOD and effects

Type	Effects on central nervous system	Examples
Stimulants	Tend to *speed up* the activity of a person's central nervous system, including the brain. These drugs often result in the user feeling more alert and more energetic.	• Crack/cocaine • Methamphetamines • Amphetamines • Nicotine • Caffeine
Depressants	They affect the central nervous system by *slowing down* the messages between the brain and the body. They affect concentration and coordination and can slow down the person's ability to respond to unexpected situations.	• Alcohol • Major tranquillisers • Benzodiazepines (e.g., Valium, Temazepam) • Volatile substances (can also be classified as other). These include glue, petrol, and paint.
Hallucinogens	Have the ability to *alter a user's sensory perceptions* by distorting the messages carried in the central nervous system. A common example is LSD (trips). Hallucinogens alter one's perceptions and states of consciousness.	• Ketamine • LSD • Datura • Magic mushrooms (psilobycin) • Mescaline (peyote cactus) • Cannabis
Opioids	Opioids act to *control pain* by depressing the central nervous system. Regular use – even as prescribed by a doctor – can produce dependence, and when misused or abused, opioid pain relievers can lead to overdose and death.	• Heroin • Morphine • Codeine • Oxycontin • Percocet • Vicodin • Fentanyl

Source: Adapted from The Department of Health (n.d.). Classification of AOD and effects. Available at: www1.health.gov.au/internet/publications/publishing.nsf/Content/drugtreat-pubs-front8-wk-toc~drugtreat-pubs-front8-wk-secb~drugtreat-pubs-front8-wk-secb-3~drugtreat-pubs-front8-wk-secb-3-2

MaVuu, T. (2020). Common drug types and what they are. Available at: https://andatech.com.au/blogs/infographics/drug-types?__hsfp=3324773745&__hssc=69956687.1.1625204801665&hstc=69956687.f102fa07a3c4a59c2ef21fc614a5327b.1625204801665.1625204801665.1625204801665.1#erid6353329

Rutgers (n.d.). Types of substances. Available at: http://aod.rutgers.edu/get-the-facts/

derivatives (codeine, methadone, etc.), and depressants (barbiturates, benzodiazepines, etc.). It must be noted that not all patterns of use discussed in this chapter necessarily fit the above definition. Therefore, we prefer the term AOD "use" instead of "abuse" on the grounds that it describes patterns of alcohol and drug use that may, or may not, be abusive. For example, having one or two drinks of alcohol after work to wind down is not "abuse" as alcohol is a central nervous system (CNS) depressant that has an initial relaxing effect, and it is commonly used for this effect. It only becomes "abuse" if these one or two drinks lead to intoxication or if the person becomes dependent on alcohol as the only way to wind down (Jackson & Sartor, 2016).

Notwithstanding the growing media coverage of kitchens and celebrity chefs, the public is perhaps less aware of the toll cooking in a commercial kitchen takes on its human resources. This chapter aims to shed light on what could be called the "dark side" of commercial kitchen life by exploring the use of alcohol and drugs by chefs, cooks, and kitchen professionals as a coping mechanism in relation to stress and the demanding working conditions.

Working in commercial kitchens

Before our investigation on the AOD use in kitchens, a brief synopsis of existing research on the life of kitchen and restaurant workers will be offered. A number of empirical studies regarding work in commercial kitchens, mainly focused on the US and UK context, can be found in the literature. These include, in the UK: Bowey (1976) and Saunders (1981a, 1981b), and in the US: Ferguson and Zukin (1998); Guyette (1981); Peterson and Birg (1988). However, it must be noted that these studies are not focused entirely on the chef's occupational context. In the UK context, the now-dated research of Chivers (1973) is dedicated entirely to the occupation of chefs and cooks. In the US context, the work of Fine (1988, 1996) is based on fieldwork carried out in the 1980s in four Minnesota restaurants. Later on, a few studies focused their attention on the culture of chefs, among which are papers on kitchen violence (Bloisi & Hoel, 2008; Giousmpasoglou et al., 2018; Johns & Menzel, 1999) and on the effects of chefs' occupational culture on hotel organisational culture (Cameron et al., 1999). Similarly, Pratten's (2003a, 2003b) papers on the retention and training of chefs and the qualities that make "a great chef", respectively, are mainly conceptual and based on limited primary data. Meanwhile, Lee-Ross (1999) investigated the core job dimensions and motivating potential of chefs in 14 UK hospitals; he found that chefs using large-scale catering systems tended to be less engaged and motivated than those using traditional cook and serve operations.

With regards to more specific kitchen-related issues, a few authors have investigated the persistent lack of female chefs in professional kitchens (i.e., Banner, 1973; Cooper, 1998; Fine, 1987; Swinbank, 2002). In addition, some insightful work has emerged on the effects of nouvelle cuisine on chefs' occupational identity and culture (i.e., Cooper et al., 2017; Rao et al., 2003; Wood, 1991) and on the trend for television and celebrity chefs (i.e., Giousmpasoglou et al., 2020; Henderson, 2011; Wood, 2000). Another stream of research investigates the skills and competencies required for chefs (i.e., Marinakou & Giousmpasoglou, 2020; Robinson & Barron, 2007; Zopiatis, 2010); this body of research suggests that a balanced approach between operational, administrative, and managerial/leadership competencies is needed for chefs in terms of career development.

It is clear from this brief overview of the "chef" literature that, although the body of knowledge about chefs has grown in recent years, the AOD use in commercial kitchens has been alluded to in a few studies.

BOX 8.1 ANXIETY IN THE KITCHEN

Many employees in the service and hospitality industries spend more time at their respective jobs than they do at home. Being forced to cover extra shifts, or voluntarily working overtime to augment the minimum wage they make, creates what the *Boston Globe* calls "a fertile ground for anxiety". With alcohol already on the premises, getting buzzed creates a much needed (if dangerous) break from the drudgery of long, late shifts, as well as a bonding experience with other like-minded employees.

Given the nature of the work, there is no change on the horizon. Customers need to be waited on at all hours, and workers know that a single bad experience can end their job (and, in the age of social media, future jobs). And yet, without any union representation, employees have no choice but to put up with the poor pay, the haphazard scheduling, and the abuse (verbal, physical, and emotional) from management. With a constant stream of potential employees waiting in the shadows to claim a newly vacated job, a worker will do anything to make sure they are still useful to the establishment. In the hospitality industry, this usually means becoming dependent on alcohol (or other drugs) to shrug off the stress and keep performing.

Managers in the hospitality industry don't have it much easier. *The New York Times* writes that "middle management is arguably the most overworked in food service", with people holding management positions usually making less than their service staff, but nonetheless working longer hours and receiving no overtime pay as a condition of their role. Their abuse of alcohol to make it through the day becomes part of the culture of employment in the industry, which augments the practice among service staff.

In 2015, the Substance Abuse and Mental Health Service Administration reported that employees in restaurants and hotels had the highest rates of substance abuse out of the entire American workforce. Twelve percent of the employees in this branch of the hospitality industry engaged in "heavy alcohol use" (consuming five or more alcoholic beverages in under two hours, for five consecutive days).

Source: adapted from American Addiction Centres (2020). Alcohol Abuse Within the Hospitality Industry. Available at: www.alcohol.org/professions/hospitality/

The role of occupational stress in AOD use

The challenging working environment described in the previous section provides fertile ground for a condition called occupational stress. The American Psychological Association (n.d.), provides the following definition for occupational stress:

A physiological and psychological response to events or conditions in the workplace that is detrimental to health and well-being. It is influenced by such factors as autonomy and independence, decision latitude, workload, level of responsibility, job security, physical environment and safety, the nature and pace of work, and relationships with co-workers and supervisors.

The literature shows a strong relationship between the occupational stress imposed by a chef's unique working environment and the consumption of alcohol and drugs. Indeed, in their study of two and three-Michelin-starred European chefs, Johnson et al. (2005) identify the high levels of stress and pressure associated with gaining a Michelin-star ranking, due to the need to consistently achieve high quality levels. In his depiction of the work environment of chefs and cooks, Fine (1988) highlights the extreme and unusual demands of the job, as do Murray-Gibbons and Gibbons (2007) who found that the consumption of alcohol and smoking help chefs to cope with occupational stress caused by a physically demanding working environment;

the top stressful factors identified were the excessive workloads, lack of performance-related feedback, and staff shortages.

In an earlier study, Rowley and Purcell (2001) reported similar findings when they examined occupational stress and burnout within the hospitality industry in Northern Ireland. Chefs scored the highest levels of burnout amongst the occupational groups surveyed. The most common coping responses included an increased consumption of foods high in sugars, fats, and caffeine, and AOD abuse. Fatigue, high emotional exhaustion, and a low sense of personal achievement were characteristic in chefs' responses. More recently, Jung et al. (2012) found a strong link between occupational stress and turnover intention in the context of the Taiwanese luxury hotel industry. Kang et al. (2010) investigated the relationship between the work environment and certified chefs' burnout in the US; their findings interestingly suggest that a supportive work environment can on the one hand improve organisational commitment and on the other hand reduce burnout and intention to quit.

The role of aggression and violence in AOD use

Workplace aggression and violence is comprised of a continuum of behaviours (Magee et al., 2017) ranging from discourtesy and disrespect, intimidation, harassment/bullying, retaliation, verbal assault, and physical aggression (Chechak and Csiernik, 2014). In commercial kitchen settings, AOD use is found to be correlated with high levels of aggression and violence among chefs (Meloury & Signal, 2014). In their paper on kitchen violence, Johns and Menzel (1999) linked aggression with alcohol abuse in commercial kitchens. They suggested that the phenomenon was widespread within the UK hospitality industry. Indeed, they argue that aggression and violence may be more widespread in kitchens than in any other workplace in the UK. They refer to kitchen violence as a mix of verbal and physical abuse, manifesting in physical and psychological impacts, including stress, strained relationships, alcoholism, and heavy smoking. Chefs' violent and bullying behaviour was attributed to the physical pressures of the job, such as the heat, the noise from machines and shouting, and the drive to maintain standards of excellence.

Kitchen violence has become deeply embedded in chefs' working culture (i.e., Alexander et al., 2012; Bloisi & Hoel, 2008; Burrow et al., 2015; Cooper, 2012; Midgley, 2005; Murray-Gibbons & Gibbons, 2007; Wood, 2000). Midgley (2005, p. 53) acknowledges the scope of the bullying problem in the industry and its likely consequences:

> Catering is a notoriously tough business with high stress levels. When
> bullying is stirred into the mix, disaster can be the result, even for those

who consider themselves psychologically robust. One of the results of a military style of management in the kitchens is that catering is an industry riven by poor health and high levels of drug abuse and alcoholism.

Midgley (2005) reports drinking to be a common coping strategy, something deeply embedded in chefs' working culture. A recent study by Meloury and Signal (2014) similarly found a link between alcohol consumption and aggression among chefs in commercial kitchens in Australia. Male line cooks appear to be more aggressive than their supervisors (i.e., sous chef and head chef) because "they are the backbone of the culinary industry, toiling in hot, cramped, fast-paced conditions to reach the head chefs high expectations" (p. 103). A similar portrait is painted by Pidd et al. (2014) who explored the extent of AOD abuse in trainee chefs in Australia and found high levels of alcohol and illicit drug use.

Interestingly, not all chefs endorse such attitudes to kitchen violence and mistreatment. For example, former Michelin-starred chef Prue Leith has accused Marco Pierre White and Gordon Ramsay of "peddling macho nonsense and bullying staff to raise their profile" (Foggo, 2006, p. 10). It is perhaps significant that it is a female chef who acknowledges and challenges the brutal management techniques that tend to endorse and perpetuate kitchen violence. As noted earlier, women are still under-represented in the realm of professional cooking (see also Chapter 6).

The role of occupational culture and deviance

Given their unique working environment and their interdependency, chefs and cooks form a distinctive occupational community (Burrow et al., 2015; Cooper et al., 2017; Mac Con Iomaire, 2008). Indeed, Bourdain (2000, p. 124), refers to chefs as a "tribe". Their unsocial working hours contribute to their exclusion from "normal" social interaction and they enjoy a deep commitment to their colleagues, a "blind, near-fanatical loyalty … under battlefield conditions" (p. 56). Bourdain also comments that a chef "never shows up late, never calls in sick, and works through pain and injury" (p. 55). In addition, communal links are reinforced by a kitchen brigade's interdependency and cooperation which generate a feeling of belongingness and community (Fine, 1996b). The existence of an occupational community is reflected notably in chefs' and cooks' propensity to socialise at the workplace or to visit the workplace on a day off (Shamir, 1981).

Fine (1996, p. 126) argues that kitchen deviance in the form of drinking is an integral part of the occupational culture: "Much that goes on in the kitchen should not be reported to the management and must be hidden from customers.... These deviant actions typically protect the organisation and the doing of work". Robinson's research (2008) corroborates this by identifying violence and AOD as the key elements of deviance in commercial kitchens. The occupational culture in this case appears to be linked directly with deviant practices such as drinking and drug use. Lee-Ross (2005) argues that this is a mechanism where the members of a given occupational group seek solidarity in their community in order to avoid stigmatisation. This contradicts the definition of employee deviance in the workplace, which is described by Robinson and Bennett (1995, p. 556) as "a voluntary behaviour that violates significant organisational norms and ... threatens the well-being of an organisation, its members or both".

Pidd et al. (2014) discovered that young chefs are heavily influenced by workplace norms regarding AOD use. The socialisation process plays a pivotal role here whereby trainee chefs are exposed to their occupational culture, including accepted norms and behaviours such as alcohol consumption and drug use. Fine (1996) notes that bonds of communality and friendship are reinforced through play and humour, as well as through the collective consumption of alcohol at the end of a shift. This tendency is accommodated by the fact that alcohol is easily available in restaurant kitchens (Belhassen & Shani, 2012; Fine, 1996; Robinson, 2008). On the other hand, according to Fine (1996, p. 130), the occupational community sets the boundaries in AOD use: "Drinking must be limited to permit the community to function. If it is, it is 'no problem'; if not, the violator is tarred with the stigma of his deviance". Robinson (2008, p. 407) sees deviant behaviours in commercial kitchens as "a statement of occupational community". This view is consistent with Lee-Ross' (2005) argument that deviance practices are used as a boundary-forming exercise in delineating occupational membership.

AOD as a coping mechanism

The atypical nature of a chef's unsociable working hours, combined with the high adrenaline and physically and mentally demanding nature of their work, are setting the scene for AOD use in commercial kitchens. Beyond the acknowledgement of the mental and physical challenges, Giousmpasoglou et al. (2018) argue that chefs have a need for coping mechanisms not commonly seen in many other occupations, which makes them susceptible to AOD use, and which can have long-term implications for health and well-being. A recent study by Roche et al. (2014) on trainee chefs coping mechanisms came to similar conclusions. The coping process has been defined in many ways, yet the dominant model accepted in the psychology literature is the transactional coping process (Kristiansen & Roberts, 2010). According to Holt et al. (2005), this is classed as a process of transaction between the individual and the environment: coping represents efforts to manage the demands that an individual appraises as taxing or exceeding his or her resources. When situations are appraised as challenging, threatening, or harmful, coping responses are required (Holt et al., 2007).

AOD use among chefs, cooks, and kitchen professionals is also associated with performance during the shift; it aids and enhances performance during service and permits a return to equilibrium following a busy service. Giousmpasoglou et al. (2018) link AOD use in commercial kitchens, to what Benton (2009) refers to as "high functioning alcoholics" (HFAs); an HFA is clinically defined as someone who is able to maintain their "outside life" – such as a job, a home, a family, and friendships, all while drinking to excess (Sharp, 2009). Many HFAs are not viewed by society as being alcoholic because they are successful in their career and personal life. These achievements often lead HFAs to deny that they have a problem; they are less likely to feel they need treatment for alcoholism and may slide through the cracks in the healthcare system because they are not diagnosed. Though the focus of this chapter is on commercial kitchens, there are clearly other highly pressurised environments where professionals use AOD to cope and to maintain or enhance performance (Belhassen & Shani, 2012; Murray-Gibbons & Gibbons, 2007; Roche et al., 2014).

Chefs are no longer allowed to drink alcohol in the kitchen during service, nor do they commonly drink alcohol during their split shifts, however, there is still a certain shared drinking culture prevalent amongst chefs when they socialise and unwind after a shift (Cooper, 2012; Giousmpasoglou et al., 2018). There is a propensity towards using alcohol to self-medicate, as a vehicle for relieving the stresses and strains that accompany their long and arduous shifts, and for restoring balance. Such drinking practices also constitute a bonding mechanism that offers a sense of togetherness. In addition, Giousmpasoglou et al. (2018) identified a normalisation of drinking among the kitchen brigade members to unwind. Even if this practice is detrimental to health, it is the coping mechanism used by chefs to deal with the stresses associated with the demanding kitchen environment.

Furthermore, a number of chefs accept or tolerate substance use as a means to stabilise or enhance job performance due to high professional standards and competition. Kitterlin and Erdem (2009), who following the interviews with ten US-based chefs, suggested that the use of illicit drugs in commercial kitchens is not necessarily negative since they maintain or enhance performance. Such a conclusion clearly overlooks the longer-term health implications of this trend towards increasing drug use. This is a "whatever it takes" attitude that overlooks the well-being of chefs, placing operational excellence above the individual. Foucault's (1977) description of normalisation comes from his understanding of how the military and penitentiary system gain control of individuals, but it can be also used to understand the alcohol and drug culture within kitchens.

BOX 8.2 "A DAILY BEER ALLOWANCE"

One of the most striking examples of the powerful reach of alcoholism in the hospitality industry comes from the United Kingdom, with Michael Quinn. Quinn was a household name for his awards and success in turning the Ritz hotel into one of London's top dining destinations. His innovative cuisine made him the head chef in some of the UK's most prestigious hotels, and he was honoured with an MBE (Member of the British Empire). He was a favourite chef of royals, celebrities, and television and radio programs around the world.

Quinn's fame and celebrity masked a devastating alcoholism problem, which was cultivated in his line of work ("we had a daily beer allowance", he wrote of an early kitchen job), and almost claimed his life when he was only 44 years old. He became homeless and lost touch with his family, lamenting in an interview that his sons never knew their father when he was a successful cook.

In 1990, Quinn stopped drinking, and discovered that professionals in the hospitality industry had no support group or network to help them with the dizzying heights that came with success. His response was to create the Ark Foundation, which spread the message of the risk and danger of alcohol and drug abuse in the hospitality business. In the foundation's first year of operations, Quinn visited 13 colleges across England and spoke about his experiences as an alcoholic in the service industry. In 2016, the foundation hosted 179 seminars, reaching 7,300 students – some as young as 16 and 17 years old – and was instrumental in creating Employee Assistance Programs for hospitality employees, where workers suffering from mental health or substance abuse problems could confidentially seek help. Quinn died in 2017, remembered as "not only a great chef, but also someone who made a real difference to the hospitality industry".

Despite greater attention being given to the problem of drinking within the hospitality business, it remains an industry where the free flow of alcohol has been integral to the bottom line for generations (and likely will be in the future). For people who suffer from the strain of the manic work, there is still a stigma about admitting to substance abuse issues in that kind of environment. Bartenders, waitstaff, and wine experts who have made the decision to not drink rarely speak up, for fear that talking about their issues suggests that they are incapable of working with alcohol at all. There are ways to get around this. Even sober bartenders are very knowledgeable about the alcohol they serve, and some restaurateurs point out that "waiters who are allergic to chocolate […] can still serve chocolate desserts".

But it comes down to a culture that celebrates excess. The idea of "recovery" is seen as a liability and an impediment to getting the job done. For those who break the cycle of alcohol abuse in the hospitality industry, being silent about their struggles is often seen as the only way to keep their job. For many others, the customers and orders never stop coming, and the alcohol is always nearby.

Source: adapted from American Addiction Centres (2020).
Alcohol Abuse Within the Hospitality Industry. Available at:
www.alcohol.org/professions/hospitality/

Conclusion

This chapter investigated AOD use in commercial kitchen settings; there is strong evidence that alcohol consumption is ingrained in the occupational culture of chefs, cooks, and kitchen professionals; this may well be traced back to the days when historically chefs were freely given alcohol in the kitchen. It was common practice for chefs to go to the pub and drink alcohol during their split shifts (Cooper, 2012). Though such drinking practices no longer exist in today's high-end commercial kitchens, literature suggests (i.e., Burrow et al., 2015; Giousmpasoglou et al., 2018; Murray-Gibbons & Gibbons, 2007) that there is still a shared drinking culture amongst chefs, with alcohol being used to help them to socialise and to cope with the highly pressurised and stressful nature of their job. Alcohol is also used to regain balance following the "rush" of a busy service (as is marijuana, increasingly). Alcohol is revealed to act as a group bonding mechanism with its consumption being normalised among chefs despite the negative health legacy of prolonged and sustained alcohol use. The existing studies also suggest that AOD use and its tolerance among brigade members differentiate chefs as an occupational group in their work settings (i.e., hotels and restaurants). This is consistent with Robinson's view (2008, p. 407) that deviant behaviours in commercial kitchens represent "a statement of occupational community".

On the other hand, the use of drugs, specifically cocaine and amphetamines, is used as a way to maintain performance (Giousmpasoglou et al.,

2018). The tolerance and indeed encouragement of drug use in the professional kitchen reveals a perhaps shocking subordination of the well-being of the chef to the needs of the restaurant. Performance must be maintained at all costs; the end justifies the means. This can be said to represent exploitation of the chef whose health is subordinated to the needs of the "business". The chef's own desire for and drive towards excellence makes him/her susceptible to such maltreatment. This study therefore reveals that AOD use has a dual function, both related to the nature of a chef's work. It acts as a vehicle for achieving calm after a busy service and as a means to maintain or enhance performance during service.

From the facts provided in this chapter, it is evident that the tolerance of drug use in the professional kitchen may be detrimental to organisational efficiency. Alcohol and drug use in commercial kitchens can lead to low productivity, absenteeism, high turnover, and bullying. There are also health implications to prolonged AOD use for chefs. Particularly in the higher end of the profession, many chefs experience burn-out or alcohol/drug addiction due to the highly stressful working environment. Although there are signs of change, especially in the large multinational and national chains, this study shows that the problem persists. An improvement in the work-life balance of the chef would trigger several positive changes such as increased productivity, lower staff turnover, and a reduced proclivity towards substance abuse.

Today, more than ever, there is a need for the senior management and the key industry stakeholders to intervene and actively engage by creating and implementing prevention strategies. A clear message should be sent to head chefs and their brigades that AOD use will not be tolerated before, during, or after service. The use of random drug testing among brigade members would reinforce this message (this is already common practice in the US). The involvement of Chefs' Associations and awarding bodies (i.e., the Michelin Guide, CIA, The Craft Guilt of Chefs, etc.) would also be valuable in terms of underlining the importance of AOD use prevention strategies. These stakeholders could lead awareness campaigns and contribute to the creation of national/international standards in terms of AOD use in commercial kitchens. Educating the younger generations of chefs is key to sustained change; the professionalization of the occupation and the fact that the majority of young chefs now receive some kind of education (vocational or tertiary) may help towards the eradication of the phenomenon of alcohol and drug abuse in commercial kitchens. A new-found level of professionalism at the high end of professional cooking, coupled with an elevation in the status and standing of chefs, may subvert the tendency towards alcohol and drug use, but this remains to be seen. The chef is now more visible, and for this reason, s/he may be inclined to shed the negative practices that have been for so long a part of the culture of the professional kitchen.

9 Future trends

Introduction

The commercial kitchen of the future will be a different place in terms of people management. Technological and social advancements, alongside the unprecedented consequences of the COVID-19 pandemic, will transform the workplace as we know it in the hospitality industry. The industry has demonstrated high levels of resilience to crises in the past. Nevertheless, a new approach is needed in the post-COVID-19 era to adapt to the "new normal". Innovation, creativity, and reinvention describe how hospitality businesses plan for the future; the ground-breaking industry-wide changes cannot leave people management in commercial kitchens unaffected.

DOI: 10.4324/9781003160250-9

This chapter identifies the future trends in commercial kitchen people management in five different areas:

1. New technologies and cooking methods
2. Food safety protocols and kitchen design
3. Chef retention and occupational culture change
4. New approaches in chefs' training and education
5. The role of celebrity chefs

New technologies and cooking methods

There is a high-tech element to most new commercial kitchens these days, thanks to the array of touchscreen control panels, gadgets, and digital devices that now record everything from up-to-the-second refrigeration temperatures to incoming orders placed via apps by customers.

Gary Devereaux, the executive chef of the House of Lords, runs one of the most tech-savvy catering operations in the UK, comprising two major kitchens, a couple of satellite kitchens, and a team of 55 chefs catering for 2,000 covers a day across fine dining, brasserie, staff restaurants, and banqueting formats. Yet, like many chefs of his generation, he can recall a time when a kitchen was the last place you would expect to find technology: "When I started as a commis (chef) 27 years ago, a chef didn't even have a computer — you had to cross the finance office to type out the menu" (Seymour, 2019. Since then, commercial kitchens have radically changed with state-of-the-art equipment and technological solutions that help chefs improve quality, performance, and efficiency.

One of the challenges with any new technology is educating chefs to use it in the way that best serves the organisation. "Old school" chefs are less likely to accept the introduction of new technologies and cooking methods in commercial kitchens. On the other hand, the younger generation of chefs consists of college or university graduates, which means that they are familiar with new technologies. There is also a need to update the culinary arts curriculum in colleges and higher education establishments to keep up with the technological developments in the industry (Marinakou & Giousmpasoglou, 2020). Many of these institutions use dated kitchen equipment and old-fashioned cooking methods that need to be updated.

The existing technologies in commercial kitchens are based on different platforms and patterns offered by various companies on a global scale. The "connected kitchen" concept (van Buren, 2018) is a desire for a common platform or standard that allows all pieces of equipment to be controlled from a single source irrespective of brand or manufacture. At the moment, that is not possible since the major equipment suppliers are not willing to share their patterns to create a "uniform language" for all kitchen equipment. It will take some time to persuade the manufacturers and equipment suppliers to work together and agree on universal standards in terms of programming and controlling their equipment from a single source with an optional remote control.

The evolution of cooking methods such as sous vide and molecular gastronomy techniques such as flash-freezing and cold-smoking also brought changes in commercial kitchens since the early 1990s. Sous vide cooking differs from traditional cooking methods in two fundamental ways: the raw food is vacuum-sealed in heat-stable, food-grade plastic pouches, and the food is cooked using precisely controlled heating (Baldwin, 2012). Vacuum-sealing and temperature control have several benefits in terms of flavour, quality, self-life, and food safety. On the other hand, flash-freezing is a molecular gastronomy technique and did to the process of freezing food what the microwave did to the process of cooking/heating food. During this process, food is frozen almost immediately using liquid nitrogen, allowing the water content of fruit, vegetables, and other foods to freeze without forming large ice crystals that can taint the taste and texture. Flash-freezing also prevents freezer burn, preserving the original colour of the food and boosting its final presentation (Wyndham, 2018). Thanks to food science and technological advancement, the above cooking methods and techniques are indicative and not exhaustive of the recent developments in professional cooking.

A revolutionary and yet controversial (Dankar et al., 2018) cooking method that will change commercial kitchens in the forthcoming decades is 3-dimensional (3D) food printing. The idea can be traced back to the early 2010s when NASA began researching 3D-printed food in an effort to identify the best way to feed a team of astronauts for longer missions (Lupton, 2017). Although this relatively new commercial and domestic food production method is still undergoing lab tests and industry trials, several benefits are already visible and make a stronger case for commercial use; customers can customise their food in terms of ingredients, nutrition value, size, colour, and shape (Dankar et al., 2018; Liu et al., 2017). 3D food printing can also be used for educational purposes in culinary arts and nutrition studies (Gosine et al., 2021). Furthermore, the introduction of 3D food printing will contribute to food waste control and improve sustainability in commercial kitchens (Carlota, 2019). Although the technology for 3D-printed food is already available for commercial use, the general public is not ready yet to accept this ground-breaking change in their eating habits (Lupton, 2017). On the other hand, Jonathan Blutinger, a young researcher from the Creative Machines Lab, argues that "the last revolution for food processors was the microwave and this innovation was more than 70 years ago. It's time for a new one" (Carlota, 2019).

The adoption of 3D food printers in commercial kitchens is a matter of time and will bring sweeping changes in the way we select, train, and manage chefs and kitchen workers. The younger generation of chefs is familiar with new technologies, which will speed up the introduction of new integrated technologies, cooking methods, and techniques in commercial kitchens.

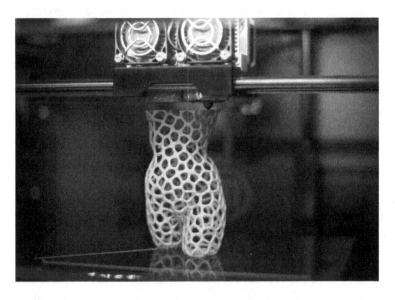

3D printing

Food safety protocols and kitchen design

The outbreak of COVID-19 has forced hotels, restaurants, cafes, and bars to adopt new hygiene and safety practices implemented by the government and the industry and alter their spaces to allow for social distancing norms. Food safety protocols have always been part of the hospitality industry standards and procedures, especially in Western countries and multinational companies operating worldwide. The national food safety-related legislation is often complemented with high industry standards;

the implementation of these standards is monitored by introducing a quality monitoring system such as the Hazard Analysis Critical Control Point (HACCP). According to the Food and Drug Administration (FDA) (2018), HACCP is a management system in which food safety is addressed by analysing and controlling biological, chemical, and physical hazards from raw material production, procurement and handling, to manufacturing, distribution, and consumption of the finished product. The majority of the pre-COVID-19 food safety procedures and protocols were designed to prevent bacterial food contamination. In the post-COVID-19 commercial kitchen environment, viral contamination will be the epicentre of kitchen professionals' attention. Making sure vegetables are chopped on a different surface to raw chicken is an obvious, age-old and straightforward principle. However, a virus that can be spread by simply breathing is a seriously challenging threat. As a result, according to James (2021), the normal practices must be reviewed and followed vigorously to keep the kitchen team members and customers safe. This, coupled with the use of masks and innovative space design, will help minimise the viral contamination risk. The post-COVID-19 era is expected to bring changes in food safety protocols and standard operating procedures (SOPs); FDA (Figure 9.1) provides

Figure 9.1 Best practices for retail food stores, restaurants, and food pick-up/delivery services during the COVID-19 pandemic. Source: FDA (2020). Best practices for retail food stores, restaurants, and food pick-Up/delivery services during the COVID-19 pandemic. Available at: www.fda.gov/food/food-safety -during-emergencies/best-practices-retail-food-stores-restaurants-and-food -pick-updelivery-services-during-covid-19

guidelines for best practices related to food handling during and post-COVID-19 pandemic. The new industry standards will affect most areas of people management in commercial kitchens (i.e., perform background health checks upon recruitment; intensify hygiene-oriented staff training and mandatory hygiene certification for kitchen staff) (Giousmpasoglou et al., 2021).

Kitchen and workflow design will also be affected in post-COVID-19 commercial kitchens. Despite the significant differences between food and beverage (F&B) provision establishments such as hotels, restaurants, bars, cafes, and contract catering, businesses will need to align their kitchen or food production space with incorporating the new norm (Shukla, 2020). Activities related to cleaning and washing, preparation and production and food pick-up will all need to have clearly defined areas, so producing innovative designs for smaller areas may be challenging. Besides designs marking out new clearly defined spaces, they will need to show sanitation points, staff training areas and kitchen and restaurant processes. The major drivers in post-COVID-19 commercial kitchen design will be operational efficiency, safety, hygiene, and adoption of technological advances and how these are used within commercial space.

Furthermore, the high demand for takeaway food delivery during the COVID-19 pandemic has accelerated the growth of the so-called cloud, ghost, or dark kitchens (Choudhary, 2019; Schaefer, 2021). The concept of ghost kitchens appeared just before the outbreak of the COVID-19 pandemic and utilises cooking facilities that produce food only for delivery and takeout with no dine-in areas (Kim, 2021). According to Euromonitor (2019), ghost kitchens and virtual restaurants could create a \$1 trillion global market by 2030. The advent of high automation concepts such as ghost kitchens in the restaurant industry will impact people management and the culinary profession: higher demand for kitchen workers/assistants and fewer chefs poses a significant threat to culinary professionals and aspiring young chefs. The employment of chefs will be focused on menu design and new product development in head or regional offices. The introduction of automation in production lines will require minimum skills from line workers, leading to de-skilling (Fine, 2008). On the other hand, it is argued that the level of de-skilling depends on the establishment type (Fraser & Lyon, 2018). For example, there is a difference in contract catering chefs' skill set compared to chefs in fine dining restaurants. The former are more likely to be affected by the increased level of automation in commercial kitchens, where it is expected to improve efficiency and reduce labour costs. On the other hand, fine dining kitchen brigades perform a combination of manual tasks, skilled craftwork, task organisation, and intellectual creativity to achieve the best possible outcome in terms of food presentation, nutritional value, and taste. This is not expected to change in high-end kitchens, even with the introduction of automation; technology will be a valuable asset towards the liberation of chefs' creativity and the betterment of their occupational culture.

Chefs' retention and occupational culture change

The glamourisation of the chef's profession through the rise of celebrity chefs, their books and TV programs (Giousmpasoglou et al., 2020) has attracted many young people into culinary training. However, existing research indicates a number of serious challenges in the education of chefs, their skills and competencies development, especially those who will occupy executive roles in the hospitality industry (Allen & Mac Con Iomaire, 2017). There is increased emphasis on food sophistication, which creates many challenges for chefs who must be competent and well-prepared to provide the best food and service to guests (Suhairom et al., 2019). For example, People 1st (2017) identified various issues on staff turnover in the chefs' occupation regarding lack of skills and problems with productivity and chef shortage, creating challenges in terms of human resource management (HRM) and operations as businesses have reportedly scaled down growth plans or others are struggling to operate effectively.

The latest statistics provide evidence of a retention problem among chefs. By 2022, 993,000 more people should be employed in the UK food sector, who will actually replace 870,000 existing employees (People 1st, 2015), creating a retention challenge. This may also impact the provision of food and food tourism products and services in the UK. The chef shortage is often seen as solely a UK problem, but many countries face similar challenges (People 1st, 2017): across the rest of Europe, there is evidence of chef shortages in The Netherlands, Germany, and France. Further afield in the US, the Bureau of Labor Statistics estimates that the US hospitality industry will need an additional 200,000 line cooks and chefs by 2025 (Moskin, 2015). A similar picture emerges in Canada with an estimate that 23,500 additional chefs will be needed between 2015 and 2035 – yet 9,000 of these jobs will go unfilled (Tourism HR Canada, n.d.). In Australia, the Australian National Tourism Labour Force Survey found that chefs were among the top five occupations projected to have the biggest skill shortages (Deloitte, 2015). More than 38,000 chefs are currently needed across

Australia. New Zealand is experiencing a similar shortage. The New Zealand Tourism Industry Association estimates that another 6,000 chefs will be required by 2025 and believes it is the biggest skill shortage facing the hospitality sector (Tourism 2025, 2015).

Recruiting for chef roles continues to be a major challenge in the sector, forcing some businesses to de-skill their operations to address the skills gap. Interestingly, the EU Skills Group (2015) reported that half of the catering colleges have seen student numbers fall on chef courses, whilst at the same time the number of chef apprentices has also fallen, reducing the potential to develop future chefs. Recruiting, training, developing, and retaining good kitchen professionals with the required competencies to work in the sector may contribute to the development and growth of food tourism in the UK as one good option to deal with Brexit and other employment issues in hospitality and tourism development in the country. Marinakou and Giousmpasoglou (2020) propose that policymakers need to adopt a more complex perception of the chefs' occupation. A chef's career campaign at different school levels could be developed to present the benefits of work in this sector. A link can also be developed with apprenticeships targeting all age groups, ethnic groups, and women.

The old way of thinking regarding the existing occupational culture should change to tackle the multifaceted issues driving the shortage of chefs. Social movements such as #metoo and #blm discussed earlier in this book (Chapter 6) create awareness and function as pressure groups towards the democratisation and rationalisation in chefs' regimental occupational culture (Giousmpasoglou et al., 2018). Furthermore, the adoption of corporate structures in F&B establishments' chains (i.e., hotels, restaurants, bars, and pubs) moves towards eradicating phenomena such as bullying, violence, and substance use in commercial kitchens. The new generation of chefs already drive this change; they are more educated, passionate, diverse, multicultural, and their career opportunities are available globally. Younger chefs are also active on social media (Giousmpasoglou et al., 2020), which are often used to report abusive and violent behaviours at the workplace. Current retention and talent management initiatives should be upscaled to maximise opportunities for students and young entrants. For example, businesses should create a quality workplace with appropriate hours and shift patterns, pay, and incentives. Poor management and aggressive and sometimes sexist cultures should be eliminated, jobs should be re-engineered, and emphasis should be placed on learning and development. HR managers and culinary curricula should include in their training and development relevant leadership development programs and training on emotional intelligence (EI) and managing people in

Figure 9.2 A holistic approach to chefs' shortage. Source: adapted from Marinakou & Giousmpasoglou (2020) and People 1st (2017)

a diverse, multicultural environment. Entrepreneurial skills could also be developed to enrich and enhance the managerial and leadership mindset of chefs. Furthermore, employee performance management systems could use "build for purpose" competencies models to evaluate chefs' performance. The way forward requires a joined-up approach with action at a business level, across the sector as a whole and by governments. Based on the above discussion, we propose a holistic approach (Figure 9.2) that focuses not only on a careers campaign but also on why we continue to lose talented chefs.

New approaches in chefs' training and education

In Chapter 4, we suggest that there is a need to review the existing curriculum in culinary arts management, emphasising more on managerial and leadership skills, as well as on emotional intelligence (EI), as existing programs were perceived to be practical and/or vocational, focusing more on cooking skills and food knowledge. Moreover, food waste management, budgeting, control, knowledge of IT, and sustainability are other key operational competencies that should be included in the modules and learning outcomes offered in Higher Education (HE). Young chef trainees should also be clearly informed about working conditions and expectations in the industry. Practitioners should maintain contact with the delivery of education and training to young chefs to ensure the competencies required are developed in pre-employment. Furthermore, attendance on vocational or HE culinary arts programs should be combined with on-the-job training and learning at work.

Table 9.1 The future dynamics of culinary education across Europe

Skills currently lacking (& relevant to the future)	Communication skills were the most cited skill currently lacking, followed by special diets and then team-working skills. Social media skills, robotisation, and the use of ICT were all similarly mentioned. The skills and competencies that are needed in uncertain and changing operating environments were also explored: greater flexibility rated the highest, followed by multi-tasking. Language skills and entrepreneurial attitude were similarly (highly) cited.
Cooks' job in the future	When asked to describe the cook's job in the future, words such as *"demanding, challenging, independent, versatile, creative and expert"* all featured strongly. However, *"Technology"* appeared the most frequently used word. Staying on top of trends and managing special diets were also highlighted. Commentary included that the job would basically stay the same, but it would become more challenging *"a technician who knows how to use a knife but also the latest technology"*, *"a multi-disciplinary specialist with traditional chef skills but also much more"*, *"a business head, but be an artist with food from all over the world"*.
Skills for the future	When asked to identify the skills needed and responsibilities of a cook in the future, basic skills were prominently identified, with *communication, passion, creativity, taking responsibility, social skills,* and *computer skills* also featuring. Respondents were very vocal about the need to instil the basic knowledge and skills, including *"sources of food, process and technique, taste, taste, taste… create a memory chip of ingredients and flavours"*.
Changes in the next 10 years	Participants were asked to predict how the work of the restaurant industry will change in the next ten years. Again, *technology* featured highly, but new themes emerged such as *work-life balance, vegetarian food, raw materials* and *organic food* all coming to the fore. *Social media* and a *focus on customer service* and *personalised service* also emerged.
Skills after 2030	When asked to identify Skills after 2030, *Technology* appeared most prominently, with comments such as *"programming equipment to do time-consuming jobs"*, *"management of robots"*, and *"understanding technology and robotics"*. Technical skills still featured strongly by 2030 with ICT, *sustainability, waste management,* and *creativity* coming to the fore as opposed to the individual's interpersonal skills, which appeared more in the previous question. Respondents commented repeatedly on the *"simplicity and technique of cooking skills"* and *"environmental awareness, minimisation of loss, multiple use of products, innovation, professionalism, and pride"* continuing to be relevant by 2030.

(Continued)

Table 9.1 (Continued)

AUTOMATION	When asked to identify at what stage of work procedures could be used, *automation/technology, preparation, customer service*, and *ordering* were the top three responses. As the shortage of chefs is identified as affecting processes, *ordering food, food preparation*, and *customer services* can all be enhanced through automation.

Source: adapted from Stafford, M.R. (2019). The future dynamics of culinary education across Europe – Research Results. Available from: https://cookingforthefuture.net/the-future-dynamics-of-culinary-education-across-europe-research-results/?cookie-state-change=1620888828654

This material was produced by the CORE – Cooking for the future project, 597859-EPP-1-2018-1-FIEPPKA3-VET-JO, co-funded by the Erasmus+ KA3 programme of the European Commission.

The role of experiential learning (internships) is critical for young chefs, as it provides a framework for competencies development at the academic level and practising these in actual working environments. These competencies should be integrated into the pedagogy that aligns with industry needs and may produce graduates who are leaders in the culinary industry (Marinakou & Giousmpasoglou, 2020).

CORE is a recent European Union-funded project (Erasmus+) that explored the future dynamics of culinary education across Europe (Stafford, 2019). An integral part of the project was to gain insights from senior chefs across Europe and their vision of future skills. The project's team involved partners from Finland, Estonia, Spain, and Ireland. The online survey was distributed to networks of each respective partner, with 156 respondents completing the survey. The participants in this study were professionals best placed to give insights into the future skills requirements of their profession. A range of job titles included the following: *Owner, Chef, Catering Manager, Quality Leader, Head Chef, Shift Manager, Director, Kitchen Process Expert, Production Manager, Teacher, Executive Chef, Sous Chef, Pastry Chef, Commis Chef, Development Manager, HR Manager, and Chef De Partie.* The survey findings are summarised in Table 9.1. The future skills for chefs' education and training programmes, identified from the CORE project, align to what we have already discussed in this book: improve interpersonal skills, enhance management and leadership, and integrate sophisticated technology in the culinary curriculum.

The role of celebrity chefs

The celebrity chef is a phenomenon of contemporary popular culture that shows no sign of decreasing in interest, as reflected in the boom in TV

Figure 9.3 Celebrity chefs' social media accounts. Source: Giousmpasoglou et al. (2020, p. 3)

cookery programmes and various bestselling cookery books and chef biographies and autobiographies. The younger generation of celebrity chefs is also very active on social media (Figure 9.3). This has contributed to the professionalisation of the industry and a growing influence of the celebrity chef on consumer food habits and choices. Giousmpasoglou et al. (2020) identified a variety of roles played by the celebrity chef: the media performer, the writer, the entrepreneur, the role model, and finally, the rebel. We focus below on celebrity chefs as role models for young chefs and their substantial role in people management in commercial kitchens.

It is often argued that the phenomenon of the celebrity chef has helped to improve the image of the career as a chef, as illustrated in the rise in culinary trade school applicants (Pratten & O'Leary, 2007). Trubek (2000) argues that the advent of television and celebrity chefs in a society that values fame and individual merit has enabled chefs to claim professional status. Trubek records that, since the 19th century, chefs involved in public cooking had worked hard to fulfil the conditions for professional status by forming associations and schools, holding conferences and competitions, and consistently claiming the expert knowledge required to perform their work adequately. Still, they struggled to obtain the social, political, and economic approbation that would validate their professional claims.

Interestingly, celebrity chefs tend to come from socially and economically deprived backgrounds (Hyman, 2008) and tend to use the survival strategies learned whilst growing up to survive and thrive within the kitchen environment (Burrow et al., 2015). Indeed, the biggest influence on the restaurant industry in Britain in recent times has been Marco Pierre White (Cooper, 2012; Zopiatis & Melanthiou, 2019) (Box 9.1). His book *White Heat* was read by what became the next generation of Michelin-starred chefs, and in it, many saw somebody from their own socio-economic background who had achieved an enviable and desirable position within society, and they wanted to emulate him. As Cameron (2004) argues, it is common to hear Michelin-starred chefs, such as Marco Pierre White or Nico Ladenis, referring to their occupation as a profession. However, the latter do not refer to all chefs but primarily to those who have proved their standing in a hierarchy of high culinary skills, by progressing through the different positions of the partie system, over many years. Although professional status is likely to apply more to those adequately experienced chefs, the rising popularity of celebrity and Michelin-starred chefs can nevertheless be said to have raised the standing of the occupation and brought it close to professional status in the eyes of the public.

BOX 9.1 MARCO PIERRE WHITE

Marco Pierre White, popularly known as the Godfather of modern-day cooking, is an influential British chef and restaurateur who is dubbed as the first celebrity chef of the UK restaurant scene.

Marco Pierre White began his successful culinary career training in the kitchen of the Hotel St George in Harrogate, North Yorkshire, before arriving in London, aged 16, with £7.36, a box of books, and a bag of clothes. He began his classical training as commis under Albert Roux and Michel Roux at Le Gavroche, a period that would lead Albert to describe him as "my little lamb". Over the next few years Marco continued his training, working at La Tante Claire (now the site of Gordon Ramsay), before working in the kitchens of Raymond Blanc at Le Manoir aux Quat' Saisons and Nico Ladenis of Chez Nico at Ninety Park Lane. In 1987 Marco opened his first restaurant Harvey's in Wandsworth Common, London, where he earned his first Michelin star within a few weeks of opening. By the age of 33, Marco Pierre White had been awarded three Michelin stars, becoming the youngest Briton (at the time) bestowed with this accolade. And then, about five years later, in 1999, he famously renounced them, being the first in a row of Michelin-starred chefs who "gave back" their prestigious award.

White changed the landscape of British cooking. Before him, no one talked about food from the British Isle. He not just changed that concept but also made British food take main stage. He became an icon of British cooking and is looked upon by a whole new generation of budding chefs and restaurateurs who take inspiration from him and consider White as their "countertop muse". He has mentored numerous famed and popular chefs of the present day including Mario Batali, Gordon Ramsay, Curtis Stone, and Shannon Bennett. However, after pursuing a 17-year long career in professional cooking, White realised that his career did not provide him with adequate returns.

In 1999 Marco announced his retirement from the kitchen, concentrating instead on his career as a restaurateur. He has since appeared on numerous TV shows, most notably *Hell's Kitchen* and *MasterChef Australia*.

The emergence of the celebrity chef as a product and a brand name is used as a means of transformation and self-actualisation (Marshall,

2006). It is argued that celebrity chefs are used as role models from the industry to inspire and recruit young candidates in a sector that chronically suffers from a poor image due to poor working conditions and the way its workers are treated (Burrow et al., 2015; Cameron, 2004; Pratten & O'Leary, 2007). Jamie Oliver is a chef with the most influence on a student population (Lane & Fisher, 2015) with initiatives such as the Fifteen restaurant attracting and training young unemployed people as kitchen workers and chefs (Mentinis, 2017). Celebrity chefs are also very active as social campaigners, i.e., Raymond Blanc and Gordon Ramsay have supported Action Against Hunger (www.actionagainst-hunger.org.uk) for many years. In a recent development, a number of celebrity chefs, Michelin-starred chefs, and restauranteurs have voiced their support for a new campaign backed by Prue Leith that hopes to recruit 100 professional chefs to work in 100 state schools in the UK over the next five years (Turner, 2018).

There are also strong indications that celebrity chefs have contributed to an increase in the number of applicants to culinary arts courses in the past two decades (Zopiatis & Melanthiou, 2019). However, Pratten (2003a) observes that the glamour of the industry brought about by the advent of celebrity chefs and ubiquitous TV cookery programmes has had the effect of obscuring the hard work and level of dedication required to become a chef and "make it to the top". Pratten's research highlights that chef trainees tend to cite many of the characteristics of the kitchen work environment as their main reasons for leaving the industry: the poor working conditions (extreme heat in a cramped environment), the long and anti-social hours, poor pay, and enduring sexism. It is easy to see why these working conditions and attitudes are significant deterrents for many chef trainees, but Pratten suggests that the glamorous image of the industry is to blame for trainees' lack of awareness of the demands of "cheffing". Indeed, Zopiatis and Melanthiou (2019) show that although the reasonably high amount of students starting culinary college training indicates that the industry is healthy, the hospitality industry is currently undergoing a shortage of experienced chefs because many new entrants tend to leave the industry within a few years of on-the-job training. The higher the level of experience, the more serious the shortage – a situation which, according to Pratten, can be accounted for by the reluctance of many cooks to take on supervisory responsibilities. Becoming a sous chef or head chef indeed involves more administrative and managerial tasks, as well as more "risk and stress" (Pratten, 2003a, p. 240).

Giousmpasoglou et al. (2020) observe that the celebrity chef has a hand in changing the image of work in professional kitchens. The emergence of the celebrity chef as a contemporary phenomenon allows chefs to act as ambassadors for the restaurant industry and promoters of the culinary arts discipline and be role models for the next generation. They can also act as ambassadors for the improvement of employer/staff relations in a bid to improve employee well-being and to help to improve the management and retention of talented chefs.

Conclusion

The final chapter of this book explored the factors that will shape people management in commercial kitchens. The world is changing fast, and so is the culinary profession and its people. The variety and breadth of food and beverage establishments in the hospitality industry and beyond creates multidimensional challenges and needs for the current and future kitchen professionals. Furthermore, the changing consumer habits and needs and the growth and diversification of the restaurant industry create different skill-set needs for chefs, ranging from the de-skilled kitchen workers in ghost kitchens and quick service restaurants to highly qualified and trained Michelin-starred restaurant chefs.

This highly competitive profession struggles to create an attractive working environment with a reasonable work-life balance. The key issues responsible for the low retention rate and high chef turnover in commercial kitchens are the working conditions and people management practices. Management styles can be authoritative and ineffective in motivating and engaging a different generation of workers who expect to interact with their workplace in ways unimagined previously. Some senior chefs see it as a rite of passage, but for most junior chefs, the passion that drove them to become a chef cannot overcome the poor working conditions and long hours worked, so they leave (People 1st, 2017).

There is an urgent need for the culinary profession to rethink and modernise its working conditions and management practices. The corporate-structured establishments (i.e., national and multinational restaurant chains) have achieved that with the introduction of standard operating procedures and good management practices. On the other hand, there are still many independent operators with a toxic work environment and a culture of bullying and intimidation. When these conditions are coupled with low pay and lack of flexibility in the hours on offer (sometimes 60–70 hours per week), employee burnout or high turnover is inevitable.

In this chapter, we tried to identify the factors that will shape people management in commercial kitchens in the near future (Figure 9.4). The introduction of new technologies and new cooking methods will shape

Figure 9.4 Factors that will shape people management in commercial kitchens

and influence the future generations of chefs and commercial kitchen professionals heavily. A new set of skills will be required to cope with the demands and latest developments in culinary arts. This inevitably will lead to a change in the way chefs are trained and educated, both at vocational and higher education levels. One of the biggest challenges, nevertheless, will be to redefine the occupational culture, which is to blame for the retention problem on a global scale. There is also a need to increase diversity and multiculturism in commercial kitchens. Celebrity chefs can play a pivotal role in this process by using the media to promote the culinary profession and attract young and aspiring chefs. Nevertheless, the chef profession "rebranding" must be a collective effort that will involve all the key stakeholders (i.e., kitchen professionals, industry associations, education and training, local community, governments, etc.). The ultimate aim is to create the conditions to attract young and talented apprentices, who will set the foundations of the future chefs' and kitchen professionals' workforce.

References

Abarca, M. E. (2006). *Voices in the kitchen: Views of food and the world from working-class Mexican and Mexican American women.* Texas A&M University Press.

Acker, J. (1992). From sex roles to gendered institutions. *Contemporary Sociology, 21*(15), 565–568.

ADF (2021). Drug wheel. Retrieved from https://adf.org.au/insights/drug-wheel/

Adler, T. (2017). How female chefs are changing restaurant kitchen culture. Retrieved from https://www.vogue.com/article/rising-female-chefs-in-america -sara-kramer-sarah-hymanson-september-issue-vogue

Agg, J. (2017). *I hear she's a real bitch.* Penguin Books.

Aitchison, C., Jordan, F., & Brackenridge, C. (1999). Women in leisure management: A survey of gender equity. *Women in Management Review, 14*(4), 121–127.

Al Mamun, A., Fazal, S. A., & Muniady, R. (2019). Entrepreneurial knowledge, skills, competencies and performance. *Asia Pacific Journal of Innovation and Entrepreneurship, 13*(1), 29–48.

Albors-Garrigos, J., Haddaji, M., & Garcia-Segovia, P. (2020). Gender discrimination in haute cuisine: A systematic literature and media analysis. *International Journal of Hospitality Management, 89*, 102569. https://doi.org/10.1016/j.ijhm .2020.102569

Alderson, S. (1993). Reframing management competence: Focusing on the top management team. *Personnel Review, 22*(6), 53–62.

Alexander, M., MacLaren, A., O'Gorman, K., & Taheri, B. (2012). "He, just didn't seem to understand the banter": Bullying or simply establishing social cohesion? *Tourism Management, 33*(5), 1245–1255.

Allen, H., & Mac Con Iomaire, M. (2017). Secrets of a head chef: Exploring factors influencing success in Irish kitchens. *Journal of Culinary Science and Technology, 15*(3), 187–222.

Amer, S. (2005). Bam. *Successful Meetings, 54*(6), 52–57.

American Psychological Association (n.d.). Occupational stress. In *Apa Dictionary of Psychology.* Retrieved from https://dictionary.apa.org/occupational-stress

Anderson, K. N. (1998). *Mosby's medical, nursing and allied health dictionary* (5th ed.). C.V. Mosby.

Andilolo, I. R., & Ranteallo, I. C. (2016). Who's cooking?: Gender issues in the professional kitchen. Retrieved from https://erepo.unud.ac.id/id/eprint/2834

Archer, D. (1999). Exploring "bullying" culture in the para-military organization. *International Journal of Manpower, 20*(1/2), 94–105.

Armstrong, M. (2009). *Armstrong's handbook of human resource management practice*. Kogan Page.

Armstrong, M. (2016). *Armstrong's handbook of strategic human resource management*. Kogan Page.

Arnett, A. (2018). Enrollment at costly culinary schools shrinks. Retrieved from https://www3.bostonglobe.com/lifestyle/food-dining/2018/04/24/enrollment -costly-culinary-schools-shrinks-demand-grows-for-skilled-kitchen-workers/ B3vHZc5WCbj66w7Y57D6XO/story.html?arc404=true

Arvela, P. (2017). Kitchen ink: *Foodies, chefs and tattoos. The Conversation, 4*, 1–2.

Ashcraft, K. (2012). The glass slipper: 'Incorporating' occupational identity in management studies. *Academy of Management Review, 38*(1), 6–31.

Ashcraft, K. L. (2013). The glass slipper: "Incorporating" occupational identity in management studies. *Academy of Management Review, 38*(1), 6–31.

Ashforth, B. E. (1994). Petty tyranny in organizations. *Human Relations, 47*(7), 755–778.

Bahn, S. (2011). Community safety and recidivism in Australia: Breaking the cycle of reoffending to produce safer communities through vocational training. *International Journal of Training Research, 9*(3), 261–266.

Balazs, K. (2001). Some like it haute: Leadership lessons from France's great chefs. *Organizational Dynamics, 30*(2), 134–148.

Balazs, K. (2002). Take one entrepreneur: The recipe for success of France's great chefs. *European Management Journal, 20*(3), 247–259.

Baldwin, D. E. (2012). Sous vide cooking: A review. *International Journal of Gastronomy and Food Science, 1*(1), 15–30.

Banner, L. W. (1973). Why women have not been great chefs. *South Atlantic Quarterly, 72*(2), 193–212.

Barker, G. (2018). *200 kitchens: Confession of a nomad cook*. Independently Published.

Barrows, C. W., & Vieira, E. T. (2013). Recommendations for the development of a new operational classification system for the foodservice industry. *Journal of Hospitality and Tourism Research, 37*(3), 349–376.

Barrows, C. W., Vieira, E. T., & DiPietro, R. B. (2016). Increasing effectiveness of benchmarking in the restaurant industry. *International Journal of Process Management and Benchmarking, 6*(1), 79–111.

Barth, F. (1969). *Ethnic groups and boundaries: The social organisation of culture difference*. Allen and Unwin.

Baum, T. (2007). Human resources in tourism: Still waiting for change. *Tourism Management, 1*(28), 1383–1399.

Baum, T. (2015). Human resources in tourism: Still waiting for change? A 2015 reprise. *Tourism Management, 50*, 204–212.

Bauman, Z. (1998). *Work, consumerism and the new poor*. Open University Press.

Beck, U. (2000). *The brave new world of work*. Translated [from German] by Patrick Camiller. Polity Press.

Becker, H. S. (1951). The professional dance musician and his audience. *American Journal of Sociology*, *57*(2), 136–144.

Becker, H. S. (1963). *Outsiders: Studies in the sociology of deviance*. Free Press of Glencoe.

Belhassen, Y., & Shani, A. (2012). Hotel workers' substance use and abuse. *International Journal of Hospitality Management*, *31*(4), 1292–1302.

Benton, S. A. (2009). *Understanding the high-functioning alcoholic: Professional views and personal insights*. Greenwood Publishing Group.

Berger, P. L., & Luckmann, T. (1966). *The social construction of reality: A treatise in the sociology of knowledge*. Doubleday Publishing.

Bindu, E. S. H., & Reddy, M. V. (2013). Indoor air quality in commercial kitchens. *International Journal of Scientific Research (IJSR)* ISSN (Online), 2319–7064.

Bindu, E. S. H., & Reddy, M. V. (2016). Perception on work environment stress by cooks in commercial kitchens. *International Journal of Sciences and Research*, *5*(10), 1320–1323.

Birdir, K., & Pearson, T. E. (2000). Research chefs' competencies: A Delphi approach. *International Journal of Contemporary Hospitality Management*, *12*(3), 205–209.

Björkqvist, K., Österman, K., & Hjelt-Bäck, M. (1994). Aggression among university employees. *Aggressive Behavior*, *20*(3), 173–184.

Bloisi, W., & Hoel, H. (2008). Abusive work practices and bullying among chefs: A review of the literature. *International Journal of Hospitality Management*, *27*(4), 649–656.

Booz, Allen, Hamilton (2018). Getting on board: A model for integrating and engaging new employees. Retrieved from https://www.opm.gov/WIKI/uploads/docs/Wiki/OPM/training/Getting_On_Board__A_Model_for_Integrating_and_Engaging_New_Employees-%5b2008.05.12%5d.pdf

Bourdain, A. (2000). *Kitchen confidential: Adventures in the culinary underbelly*. Bloomsbury Publishing.

Bourdain, A. (2004). *Kitchen confidential: Adventures in the culinary underbelly*. Bloomsbury Publishing.

Bourdain, A. (2010). *Medium raw: A bloody valentine to the world of food and the people who cook*. Bloomsbury Publishing.

Bourdieu, P. (1990). *The logic of practice*. Translated [from the French] by Richard Nice. Polity Press.

Bourdieu, P. (1996). Masculine domination revisited. *Berkeley Journal of Sociology*, *41*, 189–203.

Bourdieu, P. (2001). *Masculine domination*. Stanford University Press.

Bouty, I., & Gomez, M. L. (2013). Creativity in haute cuisine: Strategic knowledge and practice in gourmet kitchens. *Journal of Culinary Science and Technology*, *11*(1), 80–95.

Bowey, A. M. (1976). *The sociology of organisations*. Hodder and Stoughton.

Boxall, P., & Purcell, J. (2016). *Strategy and human resource management*. Palgrave Macmillan.

Boyatzis, R. (1982). *The competent manager: A model for effective performance.* John Willey and Sons.

Bradt, G. (2015). Why you must make culture the centerpiece of your Onboarding program. *Forbes.* Retrieved from https://www.forbes.com/sites/georgebradt /2015/10/28/why-you-must-make-culture-the-centerpiece-of-your-onboarding -program/#59a35a8d1f90

Brown, J. N. (2005). A brief history of culinary arts education in America. *Journal of Hospitality and Tourism Education, 17*(4), 47–54.

Brubaker, R., & Cooper, F. (2000). Beyond identity. *Theory and Society, 29*(1), 1–47.

Bryan, J. H. (1966). Occupational ideologies and individual attitudes of call girls. *Social Problems, 13*(4), 441–450.

Bureau of Labor Statistics, & United States Department of Labor. (n.d.). Occupational outlook handbook, chefs and head cooks. Retrieved from https://www.bls.gov/ ooh/food-preparation-and-serving/chefs-and-head-cooks.htm

Burkitt, I. (1994). The shifting concept of the self. *History of the Human Sciences, 7*(2), 7–28.

Burrell, J., Manfredi, S., Rollin, H., Price, L., & Stead, L. (1997). Equal opportunities for women employees in the hospitality industry: A comparison between France, Italy, Spain and the UK. *International Journal of Hospitality Management, 16*(2), 161–179.

Burrow, R., Smith, J., & Yakinthou, C. (2015). "Yes Chef": Life at the vanguard of culinary excellence. *Work, Employment and Society, 29*(4), 673–681. https://doi .org/10.1177/0950017014563103

Burton, L. (2017). How to foster motivation in your restaurant employees. Retrieved from https://www.highspeedtraining.co.uk/hub/motivating-restaurant-staff/

Butler, J. (1990). *Gender trouble: Feminism and the subversion of identity.* Routledge.

Butler, S. R., & Skipper, J. (1981). Working for tips: An examination of trust and reciprocity in a secondary relationship of the restaurant organisation. *The Sociological Quarterly, 22*(1), 15–27.

Cairns, J., Gardner, R., & Lawton, D. (2000). *Values and the curriculum.* Woburn Press.

Cairns, K., & Johnston, J. (2015). *Food and femininity.* Bloomsbury Publishing.

Cameron, D. S. (2004). *Organizational and occupational commitment: Exploring chefs from a cultural perspective* (Unpublished PhD Thesis). University of Surrey.

Cameron, D. S., Gore, J., Desombre, T., & Riley, M. J. (1999). An examination of the reciprocal affects of occupation culture and organisation culture: The case of chefs in hotels. *International Journal of Hospitality Management, 18*(3), 225–234.

Cano, M. (2019). Masculinity in the kitchen: Gender performance in the culinary arts industry. Open access. *Theses and Dissertations, 45.* Retrieved from https:// digitalcommons.utep.edu/open_etd/45

Carli, L. L. (2001). Gender and social influence. *Journal of Social Issues, 57*(4), 725–741.

Carlota, V. (2019). A guide to 3D printed food – Revolution in the kitchen? Retrieved from https://www.3dnatives.com/en/3d-printing-food-a-new-revolution-in-cooking/#!

Carroll, B., Levy, L., & Richmond, D. (2008). Leadership as practice: Challenging the competency paradigm. *Leadership*, *4*(4), 363–379.

Carter, S. B. (2015). Battered-child syndrome. Retrieved from http://onlinelibrary .wiley.com/doi.org/10.1002/9781118625392.wbecp133/full

Casey, C. (1995). *Work, self and society: After industrialism*. Routledge.

CEDEFOP - European Centre for the Development of Vocational Training (2012). Skill mismatch: The role of the enterprise. *Research Paper*, *21*. Retrieved from https://www.cedefop.europa.eu/files/5521_en.pdf

Cheary, M. (n.d.). How to: Deal with bullying at work. Retrieved from https://www .reed.co.uk/career-advice/how-to-deal-with-being-bullied-at-work/

Chechak, D., & Csiernik, R. (2014). Canadian perspectives on conceptualizing and responding to workplace violence. *Journal of Workplace Behavioural Health*, *29*(1), 55–72.

Chirilă, T., & Constantin, T. (2013). Understanding workplace bullying phenomenon through its concepts: A literature Review. *Procedia-Social and Behavioral Sciences*, *84*, 1175–1179.

Chivers, T. S. (1972). *Chefs and cooks: A study in the sociology of occupations* (Unpublished Ph.D. thesis). University of London.

Chivers, T. S. (1973). The proletarianisation of a service worker. *Sociological Review*, *21*(4), 633–656.

Choudhary, N. (2019). Strategic analysis of cloud kitchen–A case study. *Management Today*, *9*(3), 184–190.

Chuang, N., Yin, D., & Dellmann-Jenkins, M. (2009). Intinsic and extrinsic factors impacting casino hotel chefs' job satisfaction. *International Journal of Contemporary Hospitality Management*, *21*(3), 323–340.

The Clink Charity (2018). *The clink 2017–2018 yearbook*. Retrieved from https://theclinkcharity.org/wp-content/uploads/2018/07/The-Clink-2017-2018 -Yearbook.pdf

Cohen, A. P. (1985). *The symbolic construction of community*. Ellis Horwood.

Cole, H. (2019). How many 3 Michelin-starred female chefs are there? Retrieved from https://www.finedininglovers.com/article/how-many-female-chefs-have -three-michelin-stars

Collins, P. H., & Bilge, S. (2016). *Intersectionality*. Polity Press.

Connell, R. (2009). *Short introduction in gender* (2nd ed.). Polity Press.

Cooper, J. (1998). *A woman's place in the kitchen: The evolution of women chefs*. International Thomson Publishing.

Cooper, J. (2012). *The occupational identity and culture of chefs in United Kingdom (UK) haute cuisine restaurants* (Unpublished Ph.D. thesis). University of Strathclyde.

Cooper, J., Giousmpasoglou, C., & Marinakou, E. (2017). Occupational identity and culture: The case of Michelin-starred chefs. *International Journal of Contemporary Hospitality Management*, *29*(5), 1362–1379.

Cousins, J. A. (2019). *Food and beverage management: For the hospitality, tourism and event industries*. Goodfellow Publishers Ltd.

Crompton, R., & Sanderson, K. (1986). Credentials and careers: Some implications of the increase in professional qualifications amongst women. *Sociology*, *20*(1), 25–42.

CTFORUM (Connecticut Forum) (2009). Anthony Bourdain on celebrity chefs. Retrieved from www.youtube.com/watch?v=OR0pQcp5jYg

Cullen, F. (2012). An investigation in culinary life and professional identity in practice during internship. *Journal of Food Service Business Research*. Retrieved from: https://arrow.tudublin.ie/tourrcart/1/

Cullen, N. C. (2001). *Team power: Managing human resources in the hospitality industry*. Prentice-Hall.

Dankar, I., Haddarah, A., Omar, F. E., Sepulcre, F., & Pujolà, M. (2018). 3D printing technology: The new era for food customization and elaboration. *Trends in Food Science and Technology*, *75*, 231–242.

Davidson, M. J., & Cooper, C. L. (1992). *Shattering the glass ceiling*. Paul Chapman Publishing Ltd.

Davis, B., Lockwood, A., Alcott, P., & Pantelidis, I. (2018). *Food and beverage management* (6th ed.). Routledge.

Davis, K., Evans, M., & Lorber, J. (2006). *Handbook of gender and women's studies*. SAGE.

DeFalco, A. (2016). Dewey and vocational education: Still timely? *The Journal of School and Society*, *3*(1), 54–64.

Delekovcan, S. (2013). *Impacts of head chefs' leadership styles on job satisfaction of kitchen staff in Dublin's top gourmet restaurants* (MA dissertation). National College of Ireland, Dublin.

Deloitte (2015). Australian tourism labour force report: 2015–2020. Retrieved from https://www.tra.gov.au/Archive-TRA-Old-site/Research/View-all-publications/All-Publications/australian-tourism-labour-force-report-2015-2020

Deloitte (2020). Foodservice market monitor. Retrieved from https://www2.deloitte.com/content/dam/Deloitte/it/Documents/consumer-business/Deloitte_Foodser viceMarketMonitor.pdf

Dewey, J. (1938). *Experience and education*. MacMillan Publishing Company.

Dinakaran, U. (2015). Women chefs in Indian hospitality industry: Challenges and strategies. *Golden Research Thoughts*, *4*(7), 1–7.

Dinakaran, U. (2018). Barriers to career advancement of women chefs leading to their poor visibility in hotel industry: A study with special reference to Bengaluru. *Asian Journal of Managerial Science*, *7*(2), 32–37.

Dolasinski, M.J, & Reynolds, J. (2019). Hotel leader competencies: Industry practitioner perspectives. *Journal of Human Resources in Hospitality and Tourism*, *18*(3), 349–367.

Donaldson, M. (1993). What is hegemonic masculinity? *Theory and Society*, *22*(5), 643–657.

Donnet, P. A. (2008). *La saga Michelin*. Seuil.

Donou (2019). Available at: https://greekfoodnews.com/asimakis-chaniotis-the-youngest-greek-chef-with-a-michelin-star/

Douglas, M. (1982). Introduction to grid/group analysis. In M. Douglas (Ed.), *Essays in the sociology of perception* (pp. 1–8). Routledge and Kegan Paul/Russell Sage Foundation.

Eagly, A. H., & Carli, L. L. (2003). The female leadership advantage: An evaluation of the evidence. *Leadership Quarterly*, *14*(6), 807–834.

Earth Summit (2002). Gender & tourism: Women's employment and participation in tourism. Retrieved from http://www.earthsummit2002.org/toolkits/women/current/gendertourismrep.html

Einarsen, S. (1999). The nature and causes of bullying. *International Journal of Manpower*, *20*(1/2), 16–27.

Einarsen, S., Hoel, H., Zapf, D., & Cooper, C. L. (2011). The concept of bullying and harassment at work: The European tradition. In S. Einarsen, H. Hoel, D. Zapf, & C.L. Cooper (Eds), *Bullying and harassment in the workplace: Developments in theory, research, and practice* (pp. 3–40). CRC Press.

Einarsen, S., & Nielsen, M. B. (2015). Workplace bullying as an antecedent of mental health problems: A five-year prospective and representative study. *International Archives of Occupational and Environmental Health*, *88*(2), 131–142.

Emms, S. M. (2005). *The modern journeyman: Influences and controls of apprentice style learning in culinary education.* Auckland University of Technology.

Eren, S., & Guldemir, O. (2017). Factors affecting the success of international awarded Turkish chefs. *International Journal of Human Sciences*, *14*(3), 2409–2416.

Erikson, E. H. (1980). *Identity and the life cycle.* Norton.

Escoffier, M. R. (1987). The chef in society: Origins and development. *Hospitality Review*, *5*(1), 6.

EU Skills Group (2015). Development of potential models of high level occupational standards. Retrieved from https://www.euskills.co.uk/sites/default/files/Energy%20and%20Efficiency%20NOS%20Report%20Final%20Approved%20January%202015.pdf

Euromonitor (2019). Ghost kitchens virtual restaurants and a delivery optimized future. Retrieved from https://www.euromonitor.com/ghost-kitchens-virtual-restaurants-and-a-delivery-optimized-future/report

Eurostat (2020). Employment in food supply across EU regions. Retrieved from https://ec.europa.eu/eurostat/web/products-eurostat-news/-/DDN-20200522-2

Fantozi, J. (2020). 5 key takeaways from the NRA's state of the industry report. Retrieved from https://www.nrn.com/finance/restaurant-industry-sales-will-reach-889-billion-2020-4-growth-rate-says-national-restaurant

FDA (2018). Hazard analysis critical control point (HACCP). Retrieved from https://www.fda.gov/food/guidance-regulation-food-and-dietary-supplements/hazard-analysis-critical-control-point-haccp

Ferguson, E. (2007). Michelin women. *The Guardian*. Retrieved from http://www.theguardian.com/lifeandstyle/2007/mar/25/foodanddrink.features11

Ferguson, P. P. (2004). *Accounting for taste: The triumph of French cuisine.* University of Chicago Press.

Ferguson, P. P., & Zukin, S. (1998). The careers of chefs. In R. Scapp & B. Seitz (Eds.), *Eating culture* (pp. 92–111). State University of New York Press.

Fine, G. (2008). *Kitchens: The culture of restaurant work.* University of California Press.

Fine, G. A. (1987). One of the boys: Women in male-dominated settings. In M. O. Jones, M. D. Moore, & R. C. Snyder (Eds.), *Inside organisations: Understanding the human dimension* (pp. 119–127). Sage.

Fine, G. A. (1988). Letting off steam? Redefining a restaurant's work environment. In M. S. Kimmel (Ed.), *Changing men: New directions in research on men and masculinity* (pp. 131–147). Sage Publications.

Fine, G. A. (1996a). Justifying work: Occupational rhetorics as resources in restaurant kitchens. *Administrative Science Quarterly, 41*(1), 90–115.

Fine, G. A. (1996b). *Kitchens: The culture of restaurant work.* University of California Press.

Foggo, D. (2006). Leith seethes at Ramsay bad-boy gravy train. *The Sunday Times,* 22 October, *10.*

Foucault, M. (1977). *Discipline and punish the birth of the prison.* Penguin Books.

Fox, N. (2011). Star chef, facing a suit, files for bankruptcy. Retrieved from https://www.nytimes.com/2011/04/27/dining/27zakarian.html

Fraher, A. L., & Gabriel, Y. (2014). Dreaming of flying when grounded: Occupational identity and occupational fantasies of furloughed airline pilots. *Journal of Management Studies, 51*(6), 926–951.

Franzosa, S. D. (1997). Engaging Dewey's vocationalism. In S. Laird (Ed.), *Philosophy of education* (pp. 172–175). University of Oklahoma.

Fraser, S., & Lyon, P. (2018). Chef perceptions of modernist equipment and techniques in the kitchen. *Journal of Culinary Science and Technology, 16*(1), 88–105.

Fuhrmeister, C. (2015). Anthony Bourdain hits back at Donald Trump, defends immigrants. Retrieved from https://www.eater.com/2015/10/29/9638304/anthony-bourdain-donald-trumpimmigration

Fuller, J. (1981). *Professional kitchen management.* Batsford Academic and Educational.

Gay, K. (2017). *Celebrity chefs: Anne Burrell.* Enslow Publishing.

Gersh, I. (2016). Culinary industry practitioners' and educators' perceptions of core competencies for a 4-year bachelor's degree in the culinary arts. *Journal of Hospitality and Tourism Education, 28*(1), 32–43.

Gherardi, S. (1994). The gender we think, the gender we do in our everyday organisational lives. *Human Relations, 47*(6), 591–610.

Gherardi, S., & Poggio, B. (2001). Creating and recreating gender order in organisations. *Journal of World Business, 36*(3), 245–259.

Gillespie, C. (1994). Gastrosophy and nouvelle cuisine: Entrepreneurial fashion and fiction. *British Food Journal, 96*(10), 19–23.

Giousmpasoglou, C. (2012). *A contextual approach to understanding managerial roles and competencies: The case of luxury hotels in Greece* (Unpublished PhD thesis). University of Strathclyde.

Giousmpasoglou, C., Brown, L., & Cooper, J. (2018). Alcohol and other drug abuse in commercial kitchens. *International Journal of Hospitality Management, 70,* 56–65.

Giousmpasoglou, C., Brown, L., & Cooper, J. (2020). The role of celebrity chefs. *International Journal of Hospitality Management, 85*. https://doi.org/10.1016/j.ijhm.2019.102358

Giousmpasoglou, C., Brown, L., & Marinakou, E. (2019). Training prisoners as hospitality workers: The case of the CLINK charity. In *Travel & Tourism Research Association (TTRA) 2019: European Chapter Conference*. Retrieved from http://eprints.bournemouth.ac.uk/31827/1/Giousmpasoglou-Brown-Marinakou_TTRA19_conference_Final.pdf

Giousmpasoglou, C., Marinakou, E., & Cooper, J. (2018). 'Banter, bollockings & beatings': The occupational socialization process in Michelin-starred kitchen brigades in Great Britain and Ireland. *International Journal of Contemporary Hospitality Management, 38*(8), 1882–1902.

Giousmpasoglou, C., Marinakou, E., & Zopiatis, A. (2021). Hospitality managers in turbulent times: The COVID-19 crisis. *International Journal of Contemporary Hospitality Management*. https://doi.org/10.1108/IJCHM-07-2020-0741

Goffman, E. (1959). *The presentation of self in everyday life*. Doubleday Publishing.

Gomez-Mejia, L. R. (1983). Effect of occupation on task related, contextual and job involvement orientation: A cross-cultural perspective. *Academy of Management Journal, 27*(4), 706–720.

Gonzalez, C. (2019). *'Oui chef'. A sociohistorical analysis of organizational culture in the American fine dining kitchen brigade and its effects on health from 1903 to 2019* (Thesis for MSc Communication, Health, and Life Sciences, Specialization-Health and Society). Wageningen University.

Gosine, L., Kean, B., Parsons, C., & McSweeney, M. B. (2021). Using a 3D food printer as a teaching tool: Focus groups with dietitians, teachers, and nutrition students. *Journal of Food Science Education, 20*(1), 18–25.

Graham, D., Ali, A., & Tajeddini, K. (2020). Open kitchens: Customers' influence on chefs' working practices. *Journal of Hospitality and Tourism Management, 45*, 27–36.

Gray, K. (2019). 8 things you didn't know about cruise ship kitchens and food. Retrieved from https://www.insider.com/cruise-ship-kitchen-facts-2019-1

Guyette, W. C. (1981). The executive chef: Manager or culinarian. *Cornell Hotel and Restaurant Administration Quarterly, 22*(3), 71–78.

Haddaji, M., Albors-Garrigos, J., & Garcia-Segovia, P. (2017). Women chef's access barriers to Michelin stars: A case-study based approach. *Journal of Culinary Science and Technology, 15*(4), 320–338.

Harrington, R. J. (2005). Chef as CEO: An analogy and teaching tool. *Journal of Culinary Science and Technology, 4*(1), 39–52.

Harris, D. A., & Giuffre, P. (2015). *Taking the heat : Women chefs and gender inequality in the professional kitchen*. Rutgers University Press.

Hartke, K. (2018). Women chefs still walk '*A Fine Line*' in the kitchen. Retrieved from https://www.npr.org/sections/thesalt/2018/08/31/639398136/women-chefs-still-walk-afine-line-in-the-kitchen

Hegarty, J. A. (2004). *Standing the heat: Assuring curriculum quality in culinary arts and gastronomy*. The Haworth Hospitality Press.

Hegarty, J. A., & Antun, J. M. (2010). Is the chemical chef dividing culinary arts and gastronomy? *Journal of Culinary Science and Technology, 8*(2), 73–76.

Henderson, J. C. (2011). Celebrity chefs: Expanding empires. *British Food Journal, 113*(5), 613–624.

Herkes, E., & Redden, G. (2017). Misterchef? Cooks, chefs and gender in MasterChef Australia. *Open Cultural Studies, 1*(1), 125–139.

Hertzman, J., & Ackerman, R. (2010). Evaluating quality in associate degree culinary arts programs. *Quality Assurance in Education, 18*(3), 209–226.

Hertzman, J., & Stefanelli, J. (2005). *A pilot study of educators' and chefs' perceptions of the importance of subjects taught in, and factors indicating the quality of, associate degree in culinary arts programs*. University of Las Vegas, William, F., & Harrah College of Hotel. Administration. Retrieved from www.unlv.edu/faculty/jhertzman/T1HE05.htm

Hertzman, J. L., & Maas, J. (2012). The value of culinary education: Evaluating educational costs, job placement outcomes, and satisfaction with value of associate degree culinary and baking arts program graduates. *Journal of Culinary Science and Technology, 10*(1), 53–74.

Hertzman, J. L., & Stefanelli, J. M. (2008). Developing quality indicators for associate degree culinary arts programs: A survey of educators and industry chefs. *Journal of Quality Assurance in Hospitality and Tourism, 9*(2), 135–158.

Hill, T. (2020). Covid-19 impact on foodservice – And consumer insights on technology in Asia. Key insights from GlobalData's Consume Surveys and special Covid-19 reports. Retrieved from https://www.foodnhotelasia.com%2Fwp-content%2Fuploads%2FCovid-19-impact-on-foodservice-and-consumer-preferences-in-Asia-1.pdf

Hoel, H., & Salin, D. (2003). Organisational antecedents of workplace bullying. In S. Einarsen, H. Hoel, D. Zapf, & C. Cooper (Eds.), *Bullying and harassment in the workplace: Developments in theory, research, and practice* (pp. 203–218). CRC Press.

Hofstede, G., Neuijen, B., Ohayv, D. D., & Sanders, G. (1990). Measuring organisational cultures: A qualitative and quantitative study across twenty cases. *Administrative Science Quarterly, 35*(2), 286–316.

Holt, N. L., Berg, K. J., & Tamminen, K. (2007). Tales of the unexpected: Coping among female collegiate volleyball players. *Research Quarterly for Exercise and Sport, 78*(2), 117–132.

Holt, N. L., Hoar, S. D., & Fraser, S. N. (2005). How does coping change with development? A review of childhood adolescent sport coping research. *European Journal of Sport Science, 5*(1), 25–39.

Horng, J.-S., & Hu, M.-L. (2008). The mystery in the kitchen: Culinary creativity. *Creativity Research Journal, 20*(2), 221–230.

Howe, L. K. (1977). *Pink collar workers: Inside the world of women's work*. Avon.

Hu, M. L. (2010). Discovering culinary competency: An innovative approach. *Journal of Hospitality, Leisure, Sport and Tourism Education, 9*(1), 65–72.

Hu, M.-L. M., Chen, L.-C., & Lin, L. (2006). The comparative study of the culinary curriculum between Taiwan and USA. *Journal of Culinary Science and Technology, 5*(2–3), 93–107.

Huang, H. (2006). *Understanding culinary arts workers: Locus of control, job satisfaction, work stress and turnover intention.* The Haworth Press. Retrieved from http://jfbr.haworthpress.com/

Hughes, E. C. (1971). *The sociological eye: Selected papers.* Aldine-Atherton.

Hutter, M. (1970). Summertime servants: The schlockhaus waiter. In G. Jacobs (Ed.), *The participant observer: Encounters with social reality* (pp. 203–225). George Braziller.

Hyman, G. (2008). The taste of fame: Chefs, diners, celebrity, class. *Gastronomica, 8*(3), 43–52.

Jackson, K. M., & Sartor, C. E. (2016). The natural course of substance use and dependence. In K. Sher (Ed.), *The Oxford handbook of substance use and substance use disorders* (pp. 67–132). Vol. 1. Oxford University Press.

James, A. (2021). Running a hotel kitchen in a covid and post-covid world. Retrieved from https://www.hoteliga.com/en/blog/running-a-hotel-kitchen-in-a-covid-and -post-covid-world

James, K. (2002). *Escoffier: The king of chefs.* Cambridge University Press.

Jayaraman, S. (2016). *Forked: A new standard for American dining.* Oxford University Press.

Jenkins, R. (2004). *Social identity* (2nd ed.). Routledge.

Johns, N., & Menzel, P. J. (1999). "If you can't stand the heat!"… kitchen violence and culinary art. *International Journal of Hospitality Management, 18*(2), 99–109.

Johnson, C., Surlemont, B., Nicod, P., & Revaz, F. (2005). Behind the stars: A concise typology of Michelin restaurants in Europe. *Cornell Hotel and Restaurant Administration Quarterly, 46*(2), 170–187.

Johnston, R., Clark, G., & Shulver, M. (2012). *Service operations management: Improving service delivery* (4th ed.). Pearson.

Jung, H. S., Yoon, H. H., & Kim, Y. J. (2012). Effects of culinary employees' role stress on burnout and turnover intention in hotel industry: Moderating effects on employees' tenure. *Service Industries Journal, 32*(13), 2145–2165.

Kang, B., Twigg, N. W., & Hertzman, J. (2010). An examination of social support and social identity factors and their relationship to certified chefs' burnout. *International Journal of Hospitality Management, 29*(1), 168–176.

Katz, R. L. (1974). Skills of an effective administrator. *Harvard Business Review Press.* Retrieved from https://hbr.org/1974/09/skills-of-an-effective -administrator

Kay, C., & Russette, J. (2000). Hospitality-management competencies: Identifying managers' essential skills. *Cornell Hotel and Restaurant Administration Quarterly, 41*(2), 52–63.

Keller, F. J. (1948). *Principles of vocational education.* D.C. Heath and Co.

Kelly, I. (2004). *Cooking for kings: The life of Antonin carême, the first celebrity chef.* Walker and Company.

Kempe, C. H., Silverman, F. N., Steele, B. F., Droegemueller, W., & Silver, H. K. (1962). The battered-child syndrome. *JAMA*, *181*(1), 17–24.

Khomami, N. (2017). #MeToo: How a hashtag became a rallying cry against sexual harassment. Retrieved from https://www.theguardian.com/world/2017/oct/20/women-worldwide-use-hashtag-metoo-against-sexual-harassment

Kiefer, N. M. (2002). Economics and the origin of the restaurant. *Cornell Hotel and Restaurant Administration Quarterly*, *43*(4), 58–64.

Kim, H. B., & Kim, W. G. (2005). The relationship between brand equity and firm's performance in luxury hotels and chain restaurants. *Tourism Management*, *26*(4), 549–560.

Kim, S. (2021). How Covid accelerated the rise of ghost kitchens. Retrieved from https://www.cnbc.com/2021/01/15/how-covid-accelerated-the-rise-of-ghost-kitchens.html

Kitterlin, M., & Erdem, M. (2009). A qualitative assessment of employee attitudes towards pre-employment drug-testing in the full-service restaurant industry. *Consortium Journal of Hospitality & Tourism*, *14*(1), 5–21.

Kluckhohn, C. (1942). Myths and rituals: A general theory. *The Harvard Theological Review*, *35*(1), 45–79.

Kochhar, R., & Barroso, A. (2020). Young workers likely to be hard hit as COVID-19 strikes a blow to restaurants and other services sector jobs. Retrieved from https://www.pewresearch.org/fact-tank/2020/03/27/young-workers-likely-to-be-hard-hit-as-covid-19-strikes-a-blow-to-restaurants-and-other-service-sector-jobs/

Koenigsfeld, J. P., Youn, H., Perdue, J., & Woods, R. H. (2012). Revised competencies for private club managers. *International Journal of Contemporary Hospitality Management*, *24*(7), 1066–1087.

Korica, M., Nicolini, D., & Johnson, B. (2015). In search of 'managerial work': Past, present and future of an analytical category. *International Journal of Management Reviews*, *19*(2), 151–174.

Krishna, P. (2017). *NYC*'s chef of the year is a 27-year-old prodigy upending New York kitchen culture. Retrieved from https://www.thrillist.com/eat/new-york/chef-of-the-year-2017-cosme-atla-nyc-daniela-soto-innes

Kristiansen, E., & Roberts, G. C. (2010). Young elite athletes and social support: Coping with competitive and organizational stress in "Olympic" competition. *Scandinavian Journal of Medicine and Science in Sports*, *20*(4), 686–695.

Krogstad, J. M., Passel, J. S., & Cohn, D. (2018). 5 facts about illegal immigration in the U.S. Pew Research Center. Retrieved from https://www.pewresearch.org/fact-tank/2018/11/28/5-facts-about-illegal-immigration-in-the-u-s/

Krohn, D. L. (2015). *Food and knowledge in renaissance Italy: Bartolomeo Scappi's paper kitchens*. Dorset Press.

Kurnaz, A., Kurtuluş, S. S., & Kılıç, B. (2018). Evaluation of women chefs in professional kitchens. *Journal of Tourism and Gastronomy Studies*, *6*(3), 119–132.

Lam, T., Baum, T., & Pine, R. (2001). Study of managerial job satisfaction in Hong Kong's Chinese restaurants. *International Journal of Contemporary Hospitality Management*, *13*(1), 35–42.

Lane, C. (2014). *The cultivation of taste. Chefs and the organisation of fine dining.* Oxford University Press.

Lane, S. R., & Fisher, S. M. (2015). The influence of celebrity chefs on a student population. *British Food Journal, 117*(2), 614–628.

Lashley, C., & Morrison, A. J. (2000). Introduction. In C. Lashley & A. J. Morrison (Eds.), *In Search of hospitality: Theoretical perspectives and debates* (pp. xv–xvi). Butterworth-Heinemann.

Lee, N. (2014). *Celebrity chefs: Class mobility, media, masculinity* (Doctoral Dissertation). University of Sydney.

Lee-Ross, D. (1999). A comparative survey of job characteristics among chefs using large and small-scale hospital catering systems in the UK. *Journal of Management Development, 18*(4), 342–350.

Lee-Ross, D. (2005). Perceived job characteristics and internal work motivation: An exploratory cross-cultural analysis of the motivational antecedents of hotel workers in Mauritius and Australia. *Journal of Management Development, 24*(3), 253–266.

Lewin, K. (1947). Frontiers in group dynamics II. Channels of group life; social planning and action research. *Human Relations, 1*(2), 143–153.

Leymann, H. (1990). Mobbing and psychological terror at workplaces. *Violence and Victims, 5*(2), 119–126.

Leymann, H. (1996). The content and development of mobbing at work. *European Journal of Work and Organizational Psychology, 5*(2), 165–184.

Lin, L., Horng, J. S., Chen, Y. C., & Tsai, C. Y. (2011). Factors affecting hotel human resource demand in Taiwan. *International Journal of Hospitality Management, 30*(2), 312–318.

Liu, Z., Zhang, M., Bhandari, B., & Wang, Y. (2017). 3D printing: Printing precision and application in food sector. *Trends in Food Science and Technology, 69*, 83–94.

Lock, S. (2020). Restaurant industry in the UK – Statistics & figures. Retrieved from https://www.statista.com/topics/3131/restaurant-industry-in-the-united-kingdom-uk/#dossierSummary

Lock, S. (2021). Market size of the global food service industry. Retrieved from https://www.statista.com/statistics/1095667/global-food-service-market-size/

Lou, N. M., So, A. S. I., & Hsieh, Y. J. (2019). Integrated resort employee competencies: A Macau perspective. *International Journal of Contemporary Hospitality Management, 31*(1), 247–267.

Lucas, A. (2020). Pandemic accelerated an already booming market for personal chefs. Retrieved from https://www.cnbc.com/2020/10/07/coronavirus-new-demand-for-personal-chefs-as-restaurant-industry-lags.html

Lugosi, P., Lynch, P., & Morrison, A. J. (2009). Critical hospitality management research. *Service Industries Journal, 29*(10), 1465–1448.

Lupton, D. (2017). 'Download to delicious': Promissory themes and sociotechnical imaginaries in coverage of 3D printed food in online news sources. *Futures, 93*, 44–53.

Lützen, A. C. (2010). Head chefs & leadership – A study of Copenhagen's top gourmet restaurants. Retrieved from http://studenttheses.cbs.dk/handle/10417/1214

Lynch, R. (2000). High school career and technical education for the first decade of the 21st century. *Journal of Vocational Education Research, 25*(2), 155–198.

Mac Con Iomaire, M. (2008). Understanding the heat - Mentoring: A model for nurturing culinary talent. *Journal of Culinary Science and Technology*, *6*(1), 43–62.

Magee, C., Gordon, R., Robinson, L., Caputi, P., & Oades, L. (2017). Workplace bullying and absenteeism: The mediating roles of poor health and work engagement. *Human Resource Management Journal*, *27*(3), 319–334.

Magnusson Sporre, C., Johnson, I. M., & Ekström, M. P. (2015). The complexity of making a conscious meal: A concept for development and education. *Journal of Culinary Science and Technology*, *13*(3), 263–285.

Mandabach, K. H., Revalas, D., & Cole, R. P. (2002). Pioneers of American culinary education: Lessons from the depression for culinary education today. *PRAXIS, The Journal of Applied Hospitality Management*, *5*(1), 68–85.

Marinakou, E. (2012). *An investigation of gender influences on transformational leadership in the Greek hospitality industry* (PhD Thesis). University of Strathclyde.

Marinakou, E. (2019). Talent management and retention in events: Evidence from four countries. *Event Management*, *23*(4), 511–526.

Marinakou, E., & Giousmpasoglou, C. (2019). Talent management and retention strategies in luxury hotels: Evidence from four countries. *International Journal of Contemporary Hospitality Management*, *31*(10), 3855–3878.

Marinakou, E., & Giousmpasoglou, C. (2020). Chefs' competencies: A stakeholders' perspective. *Journal of Hospitality and Tourism Insights*. https://doi.org/10.1108/JHTI-06-2020-0101

Marneros, S., Papageorgiou, G., & Efstathiades, A. (2020). Identifying key success competencies for the hospitality industry: The perspectives of professionals. *Journal of Teaching in Travel and Tourism*, *20*(4), 237–261.

Mars, G. (1982). *Cheats at work: An anthropology of workplace crime*. Allen and Unwin.

Mars, G., & Nicod, M. (1984). *The world of waiters*. Allen and Unwin.

Marshall, G. (1986). The workplace culture of a licensed restaurant. *Theory, Culture and Society*, *3*(1), 33–47.

Marshall, P. D. (2006). New media-new self: The changing power of celebrity. In P. D. Marshall (Ed.), *The celebrity culture reader* (pp. 634–644). Routledge.

Martin, E. (2004). Who's kicking whom? Employers' orientations to work. *International Journal of Contemporary Hospitality Management*, *16*(3), 182–188.

Martin, J. (1982). Stories and scripts in organisational settings. In A. H. Hastorf & A. M. Isen (Eds.), *Cognitive social psychology* (pp. 255–303). Elsevier/North-Holland.

Martin, P. Y. (2006). Practicing gender at work: Further thoughts on reflexivity. *Gender, Work and Organisation*, *13*(3), 254–276.

Mathisen, G. E., Einarsen, S., & Mykletun, R. (2008). The occurrences and correlates of bullying and harassment in the restaurant sector. *Scandinavian Journal of Psychology*, *49*(1), 59–68.

MaVuu, T. (2020). Common drug types and what they are. Retrieved from https://andatech.com.au/blogs/infographics/drug-types?__hsfp=3324773745&__hssc

=69956687.1.1625204801665&hstc=69956687.f102fa07a3c4a59c2ef21fc614
a5327b.1625204801665.1625204801665.1625204801665.1#erid6353329

McClelland, D. C. (1973). Testing for competence rather than for "intelligence." *American Psychologist, 28*(1), 1.

Mead, G. H. (1934). *Mind, self and society from the standpoint of a social behaviourist*. Edited, and with an introduction by Charles W. Morris. University of Chicago Press.

Meloury, J., & Signal, T. (2014). "When the plate is full": Aggression among chefs. *International Journal of Hospitality Management, 41*, 97–103.

Mennell, S. (1996). *All manners of food: Eating and taste in England and France from the Middle Ages to the present*. University of Illinois Press.

Mentinis, M. (2017). Romanticised chefs and the psychopolitics of gastroporn. *Culture and Psychology, 23*(1), 128–143.

Micaleff, J. V. (2020). State of the cruise industry: Smooth sailing into the 2020s. Retrieved from https://www.forbes.com/sites/joemicallef/2020/01/20/state-of-the-cruise-industry-smooth-sailing-into-the-2020s/?sh=5fd7069465fa

Michelin (2006). *Michelin guide Deutschland 2006*. Michelin Travel Publications.

Michelin (2017). Highlights: 2017 annual results. Retrieved from https://www.michelin.com%2F documents%2F2017-michelin-highlights

Midgley, D. (2005). Stay cool in the kitchen. *Management Today*, September, 50–57.

Miles, R. (2007). Culinary education: Past, present practice and future direction. In E. Christou & M. Sigala (Eds.), *International CHRIE annual conference* (pp. 266–271). Council of Hotel, Restaurant and Institutional Education.

Mitchell, R., Woodhouse, A., Heptinstall, T., & Camp, J. (2013). Why use design methodology in culinary arts education? *Hospitality and Society, 3*(3), 239–260.

Montagna, P. D. (1971). The public accounting profession: Organisation, ideology, and social power. *American Behavioural Scientist, 14*(4), 475–491.

Moskin, J. (2015). Not enough cooks in the restaurant kitchen. Retrieved from https://www.nytimes.com/2015/10/21/dining/restaurant-kitchen-chef-shortage.html

Muller, K. F., VanLeeuwen, D., Mandabach, K., & Harrington, R. J. (2009). The effectiveness of culinary curricula: A case study. *International Journal of Contemporary Hospitality Management, 21*(2), 167–178.

Mullins, L. J. (1992). *Hospitality management – A human resources approach*. Pitman.

Murphy, B. (2015). Dark tourism and the Michelin World War I battlefield guides. *Journal of Franco-Irish Studies, 4*(1), 8.

Murphy, K. S., & Olsen, M. D. (2008). *Strategic human resource management: High performance people system as core competencies. Handbook of hospitality strategic management*. Elsevier.

Murray-Gibbons, R., & Gibbons, C. (2007). Occupational stress in the chef profession. *International Journal of Contemporary Hospitality Management, 19*(1), 32–42.

National Restaurant Association (2011). *Foundations of restaurant management and culinary arts*. Prentice Hall.

National Restaurant Association (2020). Total restaurant industry jobs. Retrieved from https://restaurant.org/research/economy/indicators/restaurant-jobs

Nordhaug, O. (1998). Competence specificities in organizations: A classificatory framework. *International Studies of Management and Organization, 28*(1), 8–29.

Northouse, P. G. (2010). *Leadership; theory and practice* (5th ed.). SAGE Publications.

Oatman, M. (2017). The racist, twisted history of tipping. Retrieved from https://www.motherjones.com/environment/2016/04/restaurants-tippingracist-origins-saru-jayaraman-forked/

Office of National Statistics (2018). Employment by occupation. Retrieved from https://www.ons.gov.uk/employmentandlabourmarket/peopleinwork/employmentandemployeetypes/datasets/employmentbyoccupationemp04

Palmer, C., Cooper, J., & Burns, P. (2010). Culture, identity, and belonging in the culinary underbelly. *International Journal of Culture, Tourism and Hospitality Research, 4*(4), 311–326.

Paoline, E. A. III (2003). Taking stock: Toward a richer understanding of police culture. *Journal of Criminal Justice, 31*(3), 199–214.

Parker, A. (2006). Lifelong learning to labour: Apprenticeship, masculinity and communities of practice. *British Educational Research Journal, 32*(5), 687–701.

Paules, G. F. (1991). *Dishing it out: Power and resistance among waitresses in a New Jersey restaurant.* Temple University Press.

People 1st (2015). The skills and productivity problem. Retrieved from http://www.people1st.co.uk/ Research-policy/Research-reports/The-Skills-and-Productivity-Problem

People 1st (2017). The chef shortage: A solvable crisis? Retrieved from https://people1st.co.uk/ getattachment/Insight-opinion/Latest-insights/21st-century-chef/Report-download/Exec-summary-_-The-chef-shortage-A-solvable-crisis.pdf/?lang=en-GB

Peterson, Y., & Birg, L. D. (1988). Top hat: The chef as creative occupation. *Free Inquiry in Creative Sociology, 16*(1), 67–72.

Pfeffer, J. (1981). Management as symbolic action: The creation and maintenance of organisational paradigms. In L. L. Cummings & B. M. Staw (Eds.), *Research in organisational behaviour: An annual series of analytical essays and critical reviews* (pp. 1–52). *Vol. 3.* JAI Press.

Pidd, K., Roche, A., & Kostadinov, V. (2014). Trainee chefs' experiences of alcohol, tobacco and drug use. *Journal of Hospitality and Tourism Management, 21*, 108–115.

Pini, B. (2005). The third sex: Women leaders in Australian agriculture. *Gender, Work and Organisation, 12*(11), 73–88.

Pizam, A. (2010). Alcoholism among hospitality employees. *International Journal of Hospitality Management, 29*(4), 547–548.

Plagianos, I. (2017). Mario Batali hit with another wage lawsuit at Babbo. Retrieved from https://ny.eater.com/2017/11/29/16716398/mario-batali-wage-lawsuit-babbo-nyc

Pratten, J. D. (2003a). The training and retention of chefs. *International Journal of Contemporary Hospitality Management, 15*(4), 237–242.

Pratten, J. D. (2003b). What makes a great chef? *British Food Journal, 105*(7), 454–459.

Pratten, J., & O'Leary, B. (2007). Addressing the causes of chef shortages in the UK. *Journal of European Industrial Training, 31*(1), 68–78.

Purcell, K. (1996). The relationship between career and job opportunities: Women's employment in the hospitality industry as a microcosm of women's employment. *Women in Management Review, 11*(5), 17–24.

Quine, L. (2001). Workplace bullying in nurses. *Journal of Health Psychology, 6*(1), 73–84.

Rainsbury, E., Hodges, D., Burchell, N., & Lay, M. (2002). Ranking workplace competencies: Student and graduate perceptions. *Asia-Pacific Journal of Cooperative Education, 3*, 8–18.

Ramsay, G. (2006). *Humble pie*. HarperCollins

Rao, H., Monin, P., & Durand, R. (2003). Institutional change in toque ville: Nouvelle cuisine as an identity movement in French gastronomy. *The American Journal of Sociology, 108*(4), 795–843.

Restaurant Opportunities Centers United (2015). *Ending jim crow in America's restaurants: Racial and gender occupational segregation in the restaurant industry*. ROC United.

Robinson, R. N. (2008). Revisiting hospitality's (Marginal Worker Thesis): A mono-occupational perspective. *International Journal of Hospitality Management, 27*(3), 403–413.

Robinson, R. N. S., & Beesley, L. G. (2010). Linkages between creativity and intention to quit: An occupational study of chefs. *Tourism Management, 31*(6), 765–776.

Robinson, R. N., & Barron, P. E. (2007). Developing a framework for understanding the impact of deskilling and standardisation on the turnover and attrition of chefs. *International Journal of Hospitality Management, 26*(4), 913–926.

Robinson, R., & Brenner, M. (2020). All these celebrity restaurant wage-theft scandals point to an industry norm. Retrieved from https://theconversation.com /all-these-celebrity-restaurant-wage-theft-scandals-point-to-an-industry-norm -131286

Robinson, S. L., & Bennett, R. J. (1995). A typology of deviant workplace behaviors: A multidimensional scaling study. *Academy of Management Journal, 38*(2), 555–572.

Roche, A. M., Pidd, K., & Kostadinov, V. (2014). Trainee chefs' experiences of stress, bullying and coping in commercial kitchens. *Journal of Health, Safety and Environment, 30*(2), 259–269.

Rogers, K. (2021). Restaurants staged nimble responses to Covid's blows in 2020, but 6 years of growth were wiped away. Retrieved from https://www.cnbc.com /2021/01/26/restaurant-industry.html

Roosipöld, A., & Loogma, K. (2014). Changes in professionalism: The case of Estonian chefs. *Professions and Professionalism, 4*(3), 780.

Rothman, R. A. (1998). *Working: Sociological perspectives* (2nd ed.). Prentice-Hall.

Rowley, G., & Purcell, K. (2001). As cooks go, she went: Is labour churn inevitable? *Hospitality Management, 20*(2), 163–185.

Salaman, G. (1986). *Working*. Ellis Horwood.

Salin, D., & Hoel, H. (2011). Organisational causes of workplace bullying. In S. Einarsen, H. Hoel, D. Zapf, & C. Cooper (Eds.), *Bullying and harassment in the workplace: Developments in theory, research, and practice* (pp. 227–244). CRC Press.

Sandwith, P. (1993). A hierarchy of management training requirements: The competency domain model. *Public Personnel Management, 22*(1), 43–62.

Saunders, K. C. (1981a). *Social stigma of occupations: The lower grade worker in service organisations*. Gower.

Saunders, K. C. (1981b). *The influence of the menu structure on social relations in the kitchen* (pp. 14–18). Hospitality, June, 14–18.

Schaefer, M. (2021). Ghost kitchens and virtual restaurants accelerated by coronavirus. Retrieved from https://blog.euromonitor.com/podcast/ghost -kitchens-and-virtual-restaurants-accelerated-by-coronavirus/

Schneiders, B., & Millar, R. (2018). Heston Blumenthal, the tax havens and the ripped-off workers. Retrieved from https://www.smh.com.au/business/ workplace/chefs-complain-about-30-000-underpayment-at-heston-blumenthal-s -restaurant-20181218-p50n0b.html

Seymour, A. (2019). Rise of the machines: Can a commercial kitchen contain too much technology? Retrieved from https://www.foodserviceequipmentjournal.com/rise -of-the-machines-can-a-commercial-kitchen-contain-too-much-technology/

Shamir, B. (1981). The workplace as a community: The case of British hotels. *Industrial Relations Journal, 12*(6), 45–56.

Sharma, S., & Sharma, R. (2019). Culinary skills: The spine of the Indian hospitality industry: Is the available labor being skilled appropriately to be employable? *Worldwide Hospitality and Tourism Themes, 11*(1), 25–36.

Sharp, R. (2009). Working hard drinking harder. Retrieved from http://www .independent.co.uk.Life-style/health-and-families/features/working-hard -drinking-harder-1763130.html

Shukla, N. (2020). The making of a post-COVID hotel kitchen. Retrieved from https://www.hotelierindia .com/design/11195-the-making-of-a-post-covid-hotel -kitchen

Simpson, R. (2006). *Gordon Ramsay: The biography*. John Blake.

Sitwell, W. (2012). *Michelin stars: The madness of perfection*. YouTube. June 06. Retrieved from https://www.youtube.com/watch?v=0f-j1ctaQqw

Smith, K., Gregory, S. R., & Cannon, D. (1996). Becoming an employer of choice: Assessing commitment in the hospitality workplace. *International Journal of Contemporary Hospitality Management, 8*(6), 3–9.

Soderquist, K. E., Papalexandris, A., Ioannou, G., & Prastacos, G. (2010). From task-based to competency-based: A typology and process supporting a critical HRM transition. *Personnel Review, 39*(3), 325–346.

Sökefeld, M. (1999). Debating self, identity, and culture in anthropology. *Current Anthropology, 40*(4), 417–447.

Spang, R. (2000). *The invention of restaurant: Paris and modern gastronomic culture*. Harvard University Press.

Stafford, M. R. (2019). The future dynamics of culinary education across Europe – Research Results. Retrieved from https://cookingforthefuture.net/the-future-dynamics-of-culinary-education-across-europe-research-results/?cookie-state-change=1620888828654

Statista (2019). Number of global ocean cruise passengers 2009–2019. Retrieved from https://www.statista.com/statistics/385445/number-of-passengers-of-the-cruise-industry-worldwide/

Stierand, M. (2015). Developing creativity in practice: Explorations with world-renowned chefs. *Management Learning*, *46*(5), 598–617.

Stockdale, J. E. (1991). Sexual harassment at work. In J. Firth-Cozens & M. A. West (Eds.), *Women at work: Psychological and organizational perspectives* (pp. 54–65). Open University Press.

Strangleman, T. (2012). Work identity in crisis? Rethinking the problem of attachment and loss at work. *Sociology*, *46*(3), 411–425.

Subakti, A. G. (2013). Overview Michelin star reputation restaurant in hospitality industry. *Binus Business Review*, *4*(1), 290–300.

Suhairom, N., Musta'amal, A. H., Amin, N. F. M., Kamin, Y., & Wahid, N. H. A. (2019). Quality culinary workforce competencies for sustainable career development among culinary professionals. *International Journal of Hospitality Management*, *81*, 205–220.

Sweeney, A. (2020). What next for professional chefs after the lockdown? Retrieved from https://www.rte.ie/brainstorm/2020/0811/1158486-professional-chefs-lockdown-covid/

Swinbank, M. (2013). Men nurturing through food: Challenging gender dichotomies around domestic cooking. *Journal of Gender Studies*, *23*(1), 18–31.

Swinbank, V. A. (2002). The sexual politics of cooking: A feminist analysis of culinary hierarchy in western culture. *Journal of Historical Sociology*, *15*(4), 464–494.

Talent Management (2018). *What is an onboarding process?* Retrieved from https://www.ibm.com/talent-management/hr-topic-hub/what-is-an-onboarding-process

Testa, M. R., & Sipe, L. (2012). Service-leadership competencies for hospitality and tourism management. *International Journal of Hospitality Management*, *31*(3), 648–658.

Tongchaiprasit, P., & Ariyabuddhiphongs, V. (2016). Creativity and turnover intention among hotel chefs: The mediating effects of job satisfaction and job stress. *International Journal of Hospitality Management*, *55*, 33–40.

Tourism HR Canada (n.d.). Labour market information: Tourism-facts. Retrieved from https://tourismhr.ca/labour-market-information/tourism-facts/

Tourism2025 (2015). People & skills 2025. Retrieved from https://tia.org.nz/assets/86eb0cde68/People-Skills-2025-November-2015.pdf

Trice, H. M. (1993). *Occupational subcultures in the workplace*. ILR Press.

Trice, H. M., & Beyer, J. M. (1984). Studying organisational cultures through rites and ceremonials. *Academy of Management Review*, *9*(4), 653–669.

Trubek, A. (2000). *Haute cuisine: How the French invented the culinary profession*. University of Pennsylvania Press.

Turner, G. (2013). *Understanding celebrity*. Sage.

Turner, C. (2018). Schools are hiring Michelin-starred chefs in new campaign backed by Prue Leith. Retrieved from https://www.telegraph.co.uk/education/2018/04/19/schools-hiring-michelin-starred-chefs-new-campaign-backed-prue/

Twachtman, J. (2017). Beyond the brigade: Redefining kitchen culture. Retrieved from http://ediblenortheastflorida.ediblecommunities.com/Beyondthe-Brigade-Behind-the-Scenes-Restaurant-Kitchen-Culture

Umbreit, W. T. (1992). In search of hospitality curriculum relevance for the 1990s. *Hospitality & Tourism Educator*, *5*(1), 71–74.

U.S. Bureau of Labor Statistics (2021). Food services and drinking places. Retrieved from https://www.bls.gov/iag/tgs/iag722.htm

Valenti, J. (2015). To eliminate sexism from the kitchen, women chefs just start their own. Retrieved from https://www.theguardian.com/commentisfree/2015/jan/15/eliminate-scxism-kitchen-women-chefs-start-their-own

Van Beek, A. (2020). How to cultivate a coaching approach to support team members. Retrieved from https://www.bizcommunity.com/Article/196/610/209819.html

Van Buren, D. (2018). The connected kitchen. *Smart Chain*, January, pp. 52–58. Retrieved from https://www.qsrmagazine.com/downloads/connected-kitchen

Van de Vliert, E. (1998). Conflict and conflict management. *Handbook of Work and Organizational Psychology*, *3*, 351–376.

Van den Berg, P. T. (1998). Competencies for work domains in business computer science. *European Journal of Work and Organizational Psychology*, *7*(4), 517–531.

Van Maanen, J. (2010). Identity work and control in occupational communities. Retrieved from http://hdl.handle.net/1721.1/69852

Van Maanen, J., & Barley, S. R. (1984). Occupational communities: Culture and control in organisations. In L. L. Cummings, & B. M. Staw (Eds.), *Research in organisational behaviour: An annual series of analytical essays and critical reviews* (pp. 287–365). Vol. 6. JAI Press.

Vanlandingham, P. G. (1995). *The effects of change in vocational, technical, and occupational education on the teaching of culinary arts in America* (Unpublished manuscript). Johnson Publishing & Wales University, Providence, RI. ERIC: ED382832, 6–9.

Vineetha, S., & Raghavan, V. (2018). Vocational training in Indian prisons. *Economic and Political Weekly*, *16*, 36–41.

Vogel, D., Sohn, A. P., & Gomes, K. (2021). Analysis of competencies models in culinary arts higher education. *Journal of Culinary Science and Technology*, *19*(2), 171–186.

Vora, S. (2020). Superstar Chef Maria Loi on the unsung Greek island. Retrieved from https://www.forbes.com/sites/shivanivora/2020/11/30/superstar-chef-maria-loi-on-the-unsung-greek-island/?sh=71f7d84a12dc

Wan, T. H., Hsu, Y. S., Wong, J. Y., & Liu, S. H. (2017). Sustainable international tourist hotels: The role of the executive chef. *International Journal of Contemporary Hospitality Management*, *9*(7), 1873–1891.

Wang, Y. F., Horng, J. S., Cheng, S. Y., & Kilman, L. (2011). Factors influencing food and beverage employees' career success: A contextual perspective. *International Journal of Hospitality Management, 30*(4), 997–1007.

Weber, M. R., Crawford, A., Lee, J., & Dennison, D. (2013). An exploratory analysis of soft skill competencies needed for the hospitality industry. *Journal of Human Resources in Hospitality and Tourism, 12*(4), 313–332.

Weick, K. E. (1979). Cognitive processes in organisations. In B.M. Staw (Ed.), *Research in organisational behaviour* (pp. 41–73). Vol. 1. JAI Press.

Wellton, L., Jonsson, I. M., & Svingstedt, A. (2019). Just trained to be a chef, not a leader: A study of head chef practices. *International Journal of Hospitality and Tourism Administration, 20*(4), 400–422.

White, M. P. (1990). *White heat*. Mitchell Beazley.

White, M. P. (2006). *White slave: The autobiography*. Orion.

Whyte, W. F. (1948). *Human relations in the restaurant industry*. McGraw-Hill.

Wilkins, J., & Hill, S. (1994). *The life of luxury*. Prospect Books.

Wilson, E. M. A. (2014). Diversity, culture and the glass ceiling. *Journal of Cultural Diversity, 21*(3), 83–89.

Wilson, E. M., & Iles, P. A. (1996). Managing diversity: Critique of an emerging paradigm. In *Proceedings of the British academy of management conference*, Aston.

Winn, J. (2004). Entrepreneurship: Not an easy path to top management for women. *Women in Management Review, 19*(3), 143–153.

Wong, E. S. K., & Heng, T. N. (2009). Case study of factors influencing job satisfaction in two Malaysian universities. *International Business Research, 2*(2), 86–98.

Wood, R. C. (1991). The shock of the new: A sociology of nouvelle cuisine. *Journal of Consumer Studies and Home Economics, 15*(4), 327–338.

Wood, R. C. (1997). *Working in hotels and catering* (2nd ed.). International Thomson Business Press.

Wood, R. C. (2000). Why are there so many celebrity chefs and cooks (and do we need them)? Culinary cultism and crassness on television and beyond. In R. C. Wood (Ed.), *Strategic questions in food and beverage management* (pp. 129–152). Butterworth-Heinemann.

Wright, S. D. (2015). *The compulcelebrity effect: Upmarket chef proprietors and compulsory celebrity* (Unpublished MSc thesis). Auckland University of Technology.

Wyndham, L. (2018). New cooking techniques emerge for a new generation of diners. Retrieved from https://totalfood.com/new-cooking-techniques-emerge-new-generation-diners/

Zapf, D., & Gross, C. (2001). Conflict escalation and coping with workplace bullying: A replication and extension. *European Journal of Work and Organizational Psychology, 10*(4), 497–522.

Zopiatis, A. (2010). Is it art or science? Chef's competencies for success. *International Journal of Hospitality Management, 29*(3), 459–467.

Zopiatis, A., Kyprianou, G., & Pavlou, I. (2011). Occupational challenges facing chefs: The case of Cyprus. *Journal of Quality Assurance in Hospitality and Tourism, 12*(2), 104–120.

Zopiatis, A., & Melanthiou, Y. (2019). The celebrity chef phenomenon: A (reflective) commentary. *International Journal of Contemporary Hospitality Management, 31*(2), 538–556.

Zopiatis, A., Theocharous, A. L., & Constanti, P. (2018). Career satisfaction and future intentions in the hospitality industry: An intrinsic or an extrinsic proposition? *Journal of Human Resources in Hospitality and Tourism, 17*(1), 98–120.

Zopiatis, A., Theodosiou, P., & Constanti, P. (2014). Quality and satisfaction with culinary education: Evidence from Cyprus. *Journal of Hospitality and Tourism Education, 26*(2), 87–98.

Index

Page numbers in **bold** denote tables, those in *italic* denote figures.

Abarca, M. E. 93
absenteeism 42, 128
abuse 16, 35, 42, 44–45, 99–100, **104**, 110, 113, 115, **118**, 119; alcohol 108, 121–123, 126–128; drug 108, 112, 122–123, 126, 128; emotional 42, 120; mental 35; physical 35, 110, 120, 122; sexual 99; substance 4, 6, 99, 110, 117, 126, 128; verbal 110, 120–122
Acker, J. 91–92
Adler, T. 94, 101
advancements 45; career 88–89; opportunities 95, 100; professional 100; social 129; technological 73, 82, 131; women's 105
Agg, J. 17
aggression 35–37, 54, 66, 94, **104**, 109–110, 113, 115, 122–123, 136
Albors-Garrigos, J. 92, 99
Alciatore, A. 57
alcohol and other drug (AOD) use 6, 117, **118**, 119–125, 127–128
alcoholism 112–123, 125–126
Alderson, S. **75**
Alexander, M. 3, 24, 30, 37, 107, 112–115, 122
Allen, H. 20, 41, 43, 46, 49–50, **76**, 78, 135
Al Mamun, A. **75**
Amer, S. 45
American Culinary Federation (ACF) 58, 65
American Psychological Association 121
Anderson, K. N. 117

Andilolo, I. R. 97
anxiety 110, 120
Apicius, F. **67**, 69
appraisals 39, **81**, 102
Archer, D. 114
Archestratus 54
Ark Foundation 126
Armstrong, M. 39–40
Arnett, A. 70
Arvela, P. 95
Ashcraft, K. L. 25
Ashforth, B. E. 110
Ashridge Business School 112
Auguste Escoffier School of Culinary Arts 5, 66, **67**
Australian National Tourism Labour Force Survey 135

Bahn, S. 60
Balazs, K. 16, 20, 47–48, 111
Baldwin, D. E. 131
Banner, L. W. 97, 120
banter 6, 94, 106–107, 113–115
Barker, G. 23
Barrows, C. W. 11, 12
Barth, F. 29
Batali, M. 31, 142
Baum, T. 73
Bauman, Z. 27
Beck, U. 27
Becker, H. S. 25, 28
behaviour 29, 36, 48, 74, **76**, 77, 91–92, 94–95, 100–102, 110, 122, 124; abusive 42, 97, 111, 136; aggressive 109–110, 113; autocratic

70; bullying 30, 107, 112, 122; changed 100; consumer 74, 82; contemptuous 107; deviant 6, 107, 124, 127; elements 77; individual 42; intimidatory 110; leadership 50; learned 112, 115; managerial **79**; masculine 95, **104**; negative 109; non-negotiable 45; ongoing 28; operational **80**, 85; organisational 42; patterns of 92, 115; qualities 84; role-model type **79**; style **75**; traits 77; turnover 41; violent 110, 136; voluntary 124

Belhassen, Y. 117, 124–125
Bennett, S. 31, 124, 142
Benton, S. A. 125
Berger, P. L. 29
Bindu, E. S. H. 43
Birdir, K. **76**
Bise, M. 97
Björkqvist, K. 109
black lives matter 6, 90, 98, 100, 136
Blanc, R. 20, 142–143
Bloisi, W. 22, 29, 35–36, 41–42, 48, 107, 110, 119, 122
Blumenthal, H. **2**, **11**, 20, 30–32, 41
Blutinger, J. 132
Boston Cooking School 58
Bourdain, A. **2**, 16–18, 34, 36, 42, 61, 94, 100, 107–109, 113, 123
Bourdieu, P. 29, 93, 98
Bourgeois, M. 97
Bouty, I. 14
Bowey, A. M. 119
Boxall, P. 39
Boyatzis, R. 74
Bradt, G. 44
Brazier, E. 97
Brexit 43, 96, 136
Brigades system 5, 38
Brown, J. N. 55, 58
Brubaker, R. 25
Bryan, J. H. 28
bullying 3, 6, 35, **104**, 106–107, *109*, 110–115, 122–123, 128, 136, 144; concept of 109; dispute-related 110–111; kitchen 30, 41, 111, 113; origins of 110; phenomena 106; physical 110; predatory 110, 113–114; prevalence of 113; problem 112, 122;

role of 113; workplace 110; *see also* behaviour
Bureau of Labor Statistics 9, 82–83, 97, 135
Burkitt, I. 29
Burrell, J. 94
Burrow, R. 3, 30, 33, 36, 106, 110–112, 115, 122–123, 127, 140, 143
business models 10, 73
Butler, J. 92
Butler, S. R. 3

Cairns, J. 62
Cairns, K. 96
Cameron, D. S. 29–30, 119, 141, 143
Cano, M. 92–93
Carême, A. 54
Carli, L. L. 92
Carlota, V. 131–132
Carroll, B. 50
Carter, S. B. 110
Casey, C. 27
catering 3–4, 10, 13, 112, 122–123, 130; colleges 136; contract 13, 134; ferry 13; industry 36, 115; systems 119; tech-savvy 130; workforce 24
CEDEFOP (European Centre for the Development of Vocational Training) 82
Chaniotis, A. 15
Cheary, M. *109*
Chechak, D. 122
Chirilă, T. 110
Chivers, T. S. 30, 119
Choudhary, N. 134
Chuang, N. 30, 45–46
The Clink Charity 60
coffee/tea shops **12**
Cohen, A. P. 29, 33, 36
Cole, H. 97
Collins, P. H. 98
community 33–34, 123–124; chef 34–35; food 10; kitchen **67–68**; local 145; occupational 36, 123–124, 127; sense of 10; support 58
competencies 5, 7, 44, 49–50, 74, 77–78, 82, 88, 120, 136–137, **138**, 139; administrative 77, **79–80**; balanced 5; categories **75–76**; culinary-specific 78, 88–89; definition of

74, 78; development 84, 135;
entrepreneurial **75**; frameworks 74,
76, 77–78, 89; generic 74; individual
50; interpersonal 75, **79–80**; job 74;
key **79**; leadership-management **79**,
81; managerial/leadership 120; meta-
76; operational 137; personal 84;
primary 78; technical 75, 77, 84
conflict 45, 54, 97; interpersonal 110
Connell, R. 91
consumer spending 9
contamination: food 133; viral 133
Cooper, B. **3**
Cooper, J. 2–4, 24–25, 29, 34–36, 41,
91–95, 109–111, 113, 115–116, 120,
122–123, 125, 127, 141
Cousins, J. A. 12–14, 16, 21
COVID-19 pandemic 7, 9, 41, 96, 103,
129, 132, **133**, 134; impact of 50;
post 73, 129, 133–134; pre- 133
creativity 5, 10, 16–18, 47, 62, **76**,
78, 85, 87, 112, 129, **138**; artistic
80; chef's 45, 135; culinary **79**;
intellectual 135
Crompton, R. 115
cuisine 14–15, 21, 97; chef de 16,
18, 20, 55; creole 57; exquisite 14;
French 55; haute **11**, 45, 93–94,
116; innovation in 55, 126; local **11**;
molecular **11**; national **11**; nouvelle
11, 23, 120
Culinary Arts Academy, Switzerland
66, **67**, 69
Culinary Institute of America (CIA) 58,
66, **67**, 103
Cullen, F. 17
Cullen, N. C. 45

Dankar, I. 131
Davidson, M. J. 94
Davis, B. 11, **12**, 13–14, 18, 21–22
Davis, K. 91
DeFalco, A. 61
Delekovcan, S. 48–49
Deloitte 10, 135
Dewey, J. 60
Dinakaran, U. 93
dining: casual 9, **12**, 13, 21; experience
23, 86; fine 4, 9–11, **12**, 13, 17, 21,
30, 100, 103, 130, 134

discrimination 6, 90, 98–100, 105
diversity 98, 100–101, **104**, 145; gender
102; issues 5; managing 86
Dolasinski, M. J. **76**
Donaldson, M. 94
Donou 15
Douglas, M. 34
Driessens, C. 57
Ducasse, A. 41

Earth Summit 94
Eaves, M. 15
education: culinary 5, 10, 53–55, 58,
59, 60–62, 64–66, 69–70, 83–84,
138; disciplines 64; experience 65;
formal 58, 69–70, 82, 85; holistic
70; hospitality 69; liberal 41, 77,
83; non-traditional 5; paradigms
62; traditional 5, 58; vocational 58,
60–61
efficiency 5, 17, 22, 130, 134;
organisational 128, 134
Efficiency Movement 17
Einarsen, S. 110
Electronic Point of Sale (EPOS) 22
Emms, S. M. 55
emotional intelligence (EI) 50, **81**,
136–137
employee benefits 39
entrepreneurial: attitude **138**;
competency **75**; initiatives 89; role
89; skills 75, 86, 89, 137
entrepreneurship 10, 62, 78, 101–102
environment challenges 10
Eren, S. 14
Erikson, E. H. 25
Escoffier, A. 5, 16, 38, 55, *57*, 66, **67**
Escoffier, M. R. 17
escuelerie (dishwasher) 18, 21
ethnicity 22, 25, 34
ethnocentric mentality 28
Euromonitor 134
Eurostat 8
EU Skills Group 136
exploitation 6, 30–31, 98, 128

Fantozi, J. 9
Farmer, F. 58
Ferguson, E. 96
Ferguson, P. P. 18, 119

Fine, G. 2–3, 30, 35–36, 95, 119–121, 123–124, 134
Flay, B. 66
Foggo, D. 123
Food and Drug Administration (FDA) 133
food safety **80–81**, 85, 131, 133; legislation 132; procedures 133; protocols 130, 132–133
foodservice: business 21, 40; industry 4, 8–12, 22, 41–42, 50, 98, 100, 102; market 9; operations 12, 21; sector 11, 13, 100
Foucault, M. 125
Fox, N. 31
Fraher, A. L. 25, 30
Franzosa, S. D. 60
Fraser, S. 134
Fuhrmeister, C. 16
Fuller, J. 1

gastronomy 54, 92, 101; art of 89; French 54; molecular **12**, 131; social 10, 60
gastro pubs **12**
Gay, K. 18
gender 5, 22, 25, 34, 36, 41, 91–93, 95–96, 98, 101; attributes 94; concept of 91; definition 91; differences 92; discrimination 105; diversity 102; equality 102; identity 91; inequality 93; issues 73, 100; neutral 94, 96; pay gap 99; pyramid 94; roles 91–92, 94, **104**; scale 95; segregation 5–6, 90–91, 93–94, 96, 98; -specific 93; stereotypes 92–93, 97, **104**, 105
Gersh, I. **76**, 78
Gherardi, S. 91–92
Gillespie, C. 55
Giousmpasoglou, C. 2–4, 22, 30, 60, 69, **76**, 107, 110, 112–114, 119–120, 124–125, 127, 134–136, 140, 143
Goffman, E. 2–3, 25, 29
Gomez-Mejia, L. R. 14, 29
Gonzalez, C. 14, 16, 17, 20–22, 92, 95–96, 99–100, 102–103
Gosine, L. 131
Graham, D. 23
Gray, K. 13

Guyette, W. C. 119

Haddaji, M. 14, 96–97, 101
Harrington, R. J. 20
Harris, D. A. 17, 18, 22, 41, 46, 93–96, 98–99, 101
Hartke, K. 102
Hazard Analysis Critical Control Point (HACCP) 86, 133
Hegarty, J. A. 61–62, 84
Henderson, J. C. 120
Herkes, E. 93
Hertzman, J. 58, 65–66, 69–70, 83
high functioning alcoholics (HFAs) 125
Hill, T. 9
Hodgson, P. 112
Hoel, H. 112
Hofstede, G. 29
Hollywood 2
Holt, N. L. 124–125
Horng, J.-S. 78
hospitality 10, 41, 69, 73, 75, 77, 117, 136; business 32, 126, 129; competency frameworks **76**; employees 45, 69, 126; environment 96; expert 86; industry 5, 7, 22, 30–32, 41, 73, 120–122, 126–127, 129, 132, 135, 143; jobs 73; literature 3, 24, 74; managers 70; operators 72; professions 69, 84; sector 136; studies 1; workforce 4; *see also* education
Howe, L. K. 3
Hu, M.-L. M. 61, **76**, 78, 89
Huang, H. 42–43
Hughes, E. C. 25
human resources 8, 41, 49, 52, 69, 119; departments (HR) 39–40, 44, 136; management (HRM) 39–42, 44, 52, 73, 86, 135; practices 40, 73
humiliation 115
Hutter, M. 3
Hyman, G. 140
identity 4, 25, 27–30, 33, 36, 53, 108; common 27; creation 33; formation 25; gender 91; group 34; individual 25; occupational 2, 4, 24–25, 27, 29–30, 92, 111, 120; problems 60; sense of 28–29, 36; symbols of 29; work *26*, 27, 29

incentives 39, 43–44, 136
induction 6, 34, 36–37, 39, 45, 107, 114–115; training 44
innovation 10, 14, 55, 62, 78, **80**, 86, 129, 132, **138**; creative 18

Jackson, K. M. 119
James, A. 133
James, K. 55
James Beard Foundation 102
Jayaraman, S. 95
Jenkins, R. 29
job satisfaction 30, 42, 44–46, 48, 52, 107
Johns, N. 30, 35, 37, 110, 112–114, 119, 122
Johnson, C. 121
Johnson & Wales University 58, 66, **68**
Johnston, R. 12
Jung, H. S. 122

Kang, B. 29–30, 33, 36, 122
Katz, R. L. **75**
Kay, C. **76**
Keller, F. J. 54
Kelly, I. **2**, 55
Kempe, C. H. 110
Khomami, N. 99
Kiefer, N. M. 54
Kim, H. B. 40
Kim, S. 134
Kitterlin, M. 125
Kluckhohn, C. 27
knowledge, skills, and abilities (KSAs) 62, 69–70, 72, 74, 77, 84–86, 89
Kochhar, R. 9
Koenigsfeld, J. P. **75**
Kold, D. 60
Korica, M. 46
Krishna, P. 103
Krogstad, J. M. 98
Krohn, D. L. 54
Kurnaz, A. 95–98

Ladenis, N. **2**, 141, 142
La Gavroche 142
Lam, T. 45
Lane, C. 46–47
Lane, S. R. 143
Lashley, C. 62

La Varenne, F. P. 54
leadership 5, 38, 43, 48–50, 70, **75–76**, 77–78, **79**, 86, 89, 97, 139; competencies 120; day-to-day 50; deficits 73; development 136; directive 49; mindset 137; perspective 5; positions 93, 99, 102; process 52; skills 5, 42, 49, 86, 137; styles 48–50, 52, 95, 101, 103; training 49; trait 50; transformational 50
Le Cordon Bleu, Paris 66, **67**, 69
Lee, N. 17
Lee-Ross, D. 119, 124
Leith, P. 123, 143
Les Dames d'Escoffier 102
Lewin, K. 29, 60
Leymann, H. 109–110
Lin, L. 40
Liu, Z. 131
Lock, S. 9
Loi, M. 103
Loiseau, B. 16
Lou, N. M. **76**
Lucas, A. 10
Lugosi, P. 62
Lupton, D. 131–132
Lützen, A. C. 49
Lynch, R. 61

Mac Con Iomaire, M. 110, 112, 123
McClelland, D. C. **75**
McFadden, A. 15
macho atmosphere 97
Magee, C. 122
Magnusson Sporre, C. 41
Mandabach, K. H. 60
Marinakou, E. 21, 42–43, 46, 48–50, **76**, 78, **79–80**, 91–92, 98, 103, 120, 130, 136, 139
market saturation 9
Marneros, S. **76**
Mars, G. 3, 34
Marshall, G. 3
Marshall, P. D. 142
Martin, E. 44
Martin, J. 27
Martin, P. Y. 92
masculinity 91–94, 97–98, **104**, 105
Mathisen, G. E. 113
Mead, G. H. 29

Meloury, J. 3, 122
Mennell, S. 92
Mentinis, M. 143
Michelin 14–16, 34; chefs 20, 48;
    Guide 14, 128; restaurant 16; star 2,
    11, **12**, 15, 41, 46, 84, 94, 97, 107,
    112, 121, 123, 141–144
Midgley, D. 110, 112–113, 122–123
Miles, R. 54
Mitchell, R. 62
Montagna, P. D. 28
Moskin, J. 135
motivation 4, 45, 52, 60, 107; employee
    43, 50, 58; factors 45–46; reward and
    performance management 39; skills
    45; staff 39, 42–43, 45
Muller, K. F. 62
Mullins, L. J. 45
Murphy, B. 14
Murphy, K. S. 40
Murray-Gibbons, R. 41, 112–113,
    121–122, 125, 127

National Restaurant Association 9,
    86, 101
New Zealand Tourism Industry
    Association 136
Nordhaug, O. **75**
Northouse, P. G. 49

Oatman, M. 22
Office of National Statistics (ONS) 96
Oliver, J. 143
onboarding 39, 44
organisational exit 39

Palmer, C. 3, 24, 29, 33, 36
Paoline, E. A. III 29
Parker, A. 54
Paul Bocuse Institute, Lyon **68**, 69
Paules, G. F. 3
Pellaprat, H.-P. 57
People 1st 135, 144
people management 1, 4–6, 11, 23, 31,
    38, 43, 129–130, 134, 140, 144–146
performance 6, 50, **76**, 114, 125, 127–
    128, 130; appraisals 39, 102; average
    74; business 43; employee 39, 42,
    48, 137; evaluation 137; front-
    stage 23; high- 44, 107; human 39;

management **80**; micro-enterprise **75**;
    organisational 48; -related feedback
    122; superior 74
Perry, N. 31
Peterson, Y. 119
Pfeffer, J. 27
Pidd, K. 4, 123–124
Pini, B. 91
Pizam, A. 117
Plagianos, I. 31
Pratten, J. D. 30, 61, 73, 94, 114, 119,
    140, 143
public houses **12**
Purcell, K. 94

Quine, L. 114
Quinn, M. 126

Rainsbury, E. **75**
Ramsay, G. **2**, **11**, 16, 20, 42, 110,
    112–113, 123, 142–143
Ranhofer, C. 57
Rao, H. 120
recruitment 39, 43–44, 86, 89, 99,
    102, 134; cost of 48; effective 43;
    elements 77; problems 41, 83;
    traditional 77
Restaurant Institute of Connecticut 58
Restaurant Opportunities Centers
    United 98–100
Robinson, R. N. 31, 33, 41–42, 120,
    124, 127
Robinson, S. L. 124
Roche, A. M. 124–125
Rogers, K. 10
Roosipöld, A. 48
Rothman, R. A. 27–28
Roux, A. 142
Roux, M. 30, 142
Rowley, G. 122

Salaman, G. 27
Salin, D. 36, 115–116
Sandwith, P. 74, **75**, 78, **79**
Saunders, K. C. 1, 25, 29, 35, 119
Scappi, B. 54
Schaefer, M. 134
Schneiders, B. 30
segregation 94, 98, 100; gender
    5–6, 90–91, 93–94, 96, 98, 105;

horizontal 94; occupational *96*; self-
28; vertical 94
self: -actualisation 142;
-aggrandisement 110; -care 10,
22; -concept 2, **76**; -conscious 2;
-constructed 30; -developmenet
76; -efficacy 45; -employment **104**;
-esteem 60, 110; -image 25, 36,
48, 110; -life 131; -management
76; -oriented **76**; professional 30;
-reflection 62; -sameness 25; sense of
25; -worth 25; *see also* segregation
sexual harassment 6, 42, 90, 99, 101
Seymour, A. 130
Shamir, B. 123
Sharma, S. 83
Sharp, R. 125
Shukla, N. 134
Simpson, R. **2**, 36
Sitwell, W. 16
Small & Medium Enterprises (SMEs) 78
Smith, K. 45
social: activism 101; advancements
129; anti- 61, 143; approbation
140; campaigners 143; change 60,
70; class 34, 36, 61, 89; customs
114; distancing 132; functions 28;
gastronomy 10, 60; hierarchies 93;
image 61; injustice 98; institution
98; interaction 4, 23, 28–29, 34,
91, 108, 123; interpreters 25;
isolation 28; lives 91; media
66, 89, 120, 136, **138**, 140, *140*;
movements 136; networks 100;
psycho- 110; rituals 91; roles 91;
science 25; settings 29; skills **138**;
status 89; structures 2, 22, 24–25,
91; thinkers 25; ties 114
socialisation 6, 23, 34, 37, 42, 98, 107,
113–116, 124
Sökefeld, M. 25
Stafford, M. R. 139
stagiaries 21
standard operating procedures (SOPs)
133, 144
Statista 13
Stierand, M. 46
stigmatisation 109, 124
Stockdale, J. E. 94
Stone, C. 142

Strangleman, T. 27
Subakti, A. G. 15
Suhairom, N. 74, **76**, 89, 135
supply chain 10
Sweeney, A. 10, 22
Swinbank, V. A. (2002). 93–95, 97, 120
Symbolic Interactionist 25

takeaway 10, **12**, 134
talent management 42, 44, 136
team building 45, 83, 103
Testa, M. R. 75, **76**
Tongchaiprasit, P. 4, 30
tourism 72–73, 75, **76**; development
136; environment 96; food 135–
136; industry 22; literature 74;
professions 84
Tourism HR Canada 135
training 5, 20, 41–45, 47–48, 53–55,
69, 74, **76**, 82, 83, 86, 89, 101,
113, 119, 130, 136–137, 142–143,
145; apprenticeship 20; classical
142; culinary 54, 66, 135, 142,
144; and development 39; diverse
20; induction 44; initiatives 82;
leadership 49; on-the-job 55,
69, 137, 143; opportunities **104**;
programmes 102, 139; specialised
57, 60; staff 39, **80**, 134; vocational
60, 66
Trice, H. M. 27–29, 36
Trist, W. 32
Trubek, A. 55, 140
Tschumi, J. 57
Turner, C. 143
turnover 48; behaviour 41; chef 41–42,
144; cost of 44, 77; employee 30,
73; high 128, 144; improved 40;
intention 43, 122; labour 45; staff
41, 43–44, 128, 135; voluntary 42,
77, 83

UK Ministry of Justice (MoJ) 60
Umbreit, W. T. **75**
University College Birmingham
(Birmingham College of Food
Tourism and Creative Studies) 69
University of Derby 69
U.S. Bureau of Labor Statistics (BLS)
9, 82–83, 97, 135

Valenti, J. 94, 101, 103
Van Beek, A. 44–45, 48
Van Buren, D. 130
Van den Berg, P. T. **75**
Van de Vliert, E. 110
Van Maanen, J. 25, 27
Vanlandingham, P. G. 58
Vatel, F. **3**, 16
vending machines 13
victimisation 109–110
Vineetha, S. 60
violence 3, 6, 30, 35, 101, **104**, 106–
    107, 110–113, 115, 122, 124, 136;
    kitchen 41, 112–113, 119, 122–123;
    physical 110; threats of 113
vocational 53, 61–62, 65, 137;
    apprenticeship 53; approach 55,
    62, 66; aspirations 60; choice
    61; culinary training 54, 61, 65;
    education 58, 60–61, 128, 145;
    institution 58, 63, 69; knowledge 62;
    nature 74, 77, 84; programmes 58,
    60; schools 63–64; training 60, 66;
    traits 61, 75
Vogel, D. 78
Vora, S. 103

wage exploitation 31
Wan, T. H. **76**, **79–80**
Wang, Y. F. 40
Washburne Trade School, Chicago 58
Weber, M. R. 77

Weick, K. E. 27
Wellton, L. 22, 43, 45–46
Westminster Kingsway College,
    London **67**
White, M. P. **2**, 16, 36, 110, 113,
    123, 141, 142
Whyte, W. F. 29
Wilkins, J. 54
Wilson, E. M. A. 91–92, 97
Winn, J. 97
Woman's Educational Association of
    Boston 58
Women Chefs and Restauranteurs
    (WCR) 102
Wong, E. S. K. 45
Wood, R. C. 2–3, 16, 24–29, 35, 112,
    120, 122
worker exploitation 6, 30
working hours: irregular 94; long 94, 97,
    104; unsocial 34, 108, 123–124
work-life balance 39, **104**, 128,
    138, 144
work stress 42–43
Wright, S. D. 2
Wyndham, L. 131

Zakarian, G. 31
Zapf, D. 110
Zeta-Jones, C. 2, **3**
Zopiatis, A. 3, 45–46, 48–50, 58,
    65–66, 73–74, **76**, 78, **79–80**, 120,
    141, 143

Printed in the United States
by Baker & Taylor Publisher Services